The ERG

Handbook

Early Praise for The ERG Handbook

Aimee provides a "notes from the field" handbook, rich with personal experience and tried-and-tested ideas. This book will support your ERG needs, whether you're starting from scratch to create the foundations and framework for a new ERG or chapter, or you're a tenured ERG leader looking for tools to strengthen and expand the impacts of your group.

> — **Anna Ettin,**
> **Global Diversity, Equity and Inclusion – Affinity Groups at Amazon**

The ERG Handbook: Everything You Wanted to Know About ERGs But Didn't Know Who to Ask is a wonderful resource for anyone wanting to understand the ins and outs of affinity groups/employee resource groups/business resource groups. Aimee Broadhurst does a wonderful job translating her more than seven years of experience into a comprehensive guide and model to help all organizations regardless of what stage they are currently in. Packed with examples of intersectional programming, facts to make the business case for the importance of ERGs, and tips on how to engage members and executive sponsors (to name a few), this book is a must-have for your ERG/DEIB toolkit!

> — **Marinda Monfilston,**
> **Yale University Office of Diversity & Inclusion**

"Aimee's real-world experience in the ERG trenches comes through like Wonder Woman charging across enemy lines. Her stories and knowledge have generated a starkly sensible model, supporting workbook collateral, and tips that unearth simple yet tested observations that will save you tons of all sorts of capital. Be you a Fortune 500 or a rapidly expanding start-up, this book is invaluable in your efforts to create top-tier cultures of inclusion, diversity, and equality."

— **Lawler Kang,**
Founder & CEO - League of Allies

"In The ERG Handbook, Aimee Broadhurst offers a comprehensive and practical perspective of every stage of the Employee Resource Group formation process, all through a passionate and authoritative lens. Complete with countless worksheets, templates, and resources, this book is nothing short of a goldmine for ERG leaders and DEI practitioners looking to elevate employee engagement and succeed in the modern workplace. Aimee's voice is one of confidence and approachability and for sure one to watch in this field."

— **Jennifer Brown,**
Founder and CEO, Jennifer Brown Consulting
Author, *How to Be an Inclusive Leader*

"This book provides insightful information not only for aspiring practitioners but experienced diversity leaders alike and is an amazing resource I'm excited to leverage. Aimee uses her practical experience to successfully guide the reader to start, manage, and grow employee resource groups. Extremely well written."

— **Yulonda Burris,**
Global D&I Initiatives Leader – PayPal

This book is a comprehensive bible for any organization, D&I professional, or ERG leader. With a thorough read – one can bypass much of the heartache that comes with learning through trial and error. Not only are you able to learn vicariously through Aimee's teachings, but she also provides many templates and worksheets to help apply those learnings.

— **Raquel Barlow,**
  Diversity, Inclusion, & Outreach Manager – Cracker Barrel

Leading an ERG takes passion and a genuine desire to support your organization and help your colleagues thrive. Balancing between your paid job and your passion job is not easy. Aimee knows this balancing act all too well. She has used her experience to craft an easy-to-read guidebook, complete with templates and worksheets, that any ERG leader can leverage to launch, grow, and develop their group effectively.

— **Jolie Thompson,**
  Manager, Communications and Employee Engagement - New York City Dept. of Education

The ERG Handbook and the Companion Workbook are for those passionate about the work of ERGs. In her book, Aimee shares what she learned through her own ERG leadership journey, along with what she learned from many other ERG leaders, executive sponsors, and members. Aimee's style is confident and approachable, and her book and companion workbook will empower ERGs to lead the charge to change workplace cultures into more Inclusive Spaces.

— **Frances Hinds,**
  Sr. Specialist, Employee Experience – Hasbro

The ERG Handbook

Everything You Wanted to Know About Employee Resource Groups, But Didn't Know Who to Ask

Aimee K. Broadhurst

Printed in the United States of America

First Printing, 2021

ISBN: 978-1-953640-01-7 (paperback)

ISBN: 978-1-953640-04-8 (Kindle edition)

Page Beyond Press™

Fishers, Indiana

www.APageBeyond.com

Ordering Information:

Special discounts are available on quantity purchases by corporations, associations, and others who purchase directly from the author. Contact CoachAimee@InclusiveSpace.com for details.

Dedication

I am dedicating this book to my Mom, Carol Wood. I am sad that you are not here to see and read it, but I know you are watching me, and I feel your presence. This book would not have been possible without the lessons you taught me. Thank you for always being my cheerleader and teaching me that it was my job to stand up and be the voice for marginalized communities. Without the lessons you instilled in me, I would not be the person I am today, and I would not have been able to impact people's lives through my ERG work and my allyship. Thanks for being my Mom. I love and miss you every day.

Foreword

"Why would you want to support ERGs when they have no money and are such an old and ineffective concept."

I heard this from several people I respect in the HR and diversity world. They had their perspective. I had my own.

As the expert on confidence science, it is neurologically provable how vital belonging is to everyone's well-being. Whenever I do a keynote or workshop, people come up to me in thankful tears as they are so relieved to learn they are not alone and that it is not unusual to feel like an alien, outsider, a weirdo. My one shot of confidence does help them fend for their confidence in otherwise hostile workplace waters. But I kept wondering what else I could do.

I kept getting calls from ERGs and quickly saw a more pervasive opportunity to deliver confidence by using my business and coaching knowledge. By helping the volunteer ERG leaders be more efficient and effective, we could help millions of members.

February 2019, I started the ERG Leadership Alliance (ELA) with a mission to bring together ERG leaders so they could collaboratively create and share ERG best practices. We ran our first in-person Symposium in July 2019 and started building ELA Online to enable an ongoing exchange of resources and connections. We planned more 2020 Symposiums and local events. Then Aimee arrived as an ELA angel bringing with her incredible knowledge and passion that has helped make ELA the 'go-to group' for concrete info to launch, grow, and sustain ERGs. We were clear ELA wasn't to talk about general D&I or even ERG strategy and intention. ELA is committed to helping ERG leaders quickly reach their full potential to help their members do the same.

Then the world was shocked to experience COVID-19 and systemic racism. If there is a silver lining in either, it was an overdue realization that it must happen respectfully and equally for people to be together safely.

ERGs and all the various pseudonyms (Business Resource Groups, Affinity Groups, Employee Networks, etc.) have become critical epicenters for workplace wellness and engagement. They are no longer the right thing to do, but they are necessary employment conditions required for recruiting and retaining talent. ERGs are essential for product marketing, sales communications, and customer support. Even investor decisions often hinge on the presence of ERGs as a clear demonstration of diversity & inclusion.

Call it an ERG renaissance or redo – we finally know ERGs are not optional. However, organizations are far from prepared. ERG leaders are overwhelmed with their day jobs, let alone their volunteer ERG responsibilities. With too little money, sponsorship, time, and training, ERG leaders are drowning, often burning out.

When a surgeon recently told me that he learned most of what he does in the operating room from watching other surgeons, I was mortified. What if the other surgeon is equally inexperienced? What if there wasn't a chance to see someone do a specific procedure? Who could they call if they had a question, or would that make everyone around them nervous? Yeah, it is frightening. ERG leaders aren't quite surgeons, but they do provide a vital role in organizational health. And yet, they don't typically go to any ERG school or get certified. They have had to absorb somehow and fearlessly wing it - until now.

And yes, I expect a few calls from those naysayers who questioned me when I claimed that ERGs make a real difference. They just needed some hands-on help, and here it is.

Alyssa Dver

Confidence Crusader. Neuro Nerd. Success Equalizer.
Chair & Founder, ERG Leadership Alliance (ELA)
CEO & Co-founder, American Confidence Institute (ACI)

Table of Contents

Introduction 3

How This Book Is Structured 6

Chapter 1 – What I Know 11

Chapter 2 – What's in a Name? 15

Chapter 3 – Why Are ERGs Important? 21

Chapter 4 – Let's Get Structured 29

Chapter 5 – The Inclusive Space™ ERG Progression Model 37

Chapter 6 – The Pillars 43

Chapter 7 – Progression Model, Pillars, and Activities 49

Chapter 8 – Preparing to Launch 61

Chapter 9 – Launch 83

Chapter 10 – Welcome Aboard Executive Sponsors......................... 93

Chapter 11 – Grow.. 103

Chapter 12 – Recruiting Your 20 Percent 111

Chapter 13 – Show Me the Money.. 121

Chapter 14 – Communicate, Communicate, Communicate 133

Chapter 15 – Tools for Your Communication Journey 139

Chapter 16 – What's Programming Got to Do with It?...................... 145

Chapter 17 – To Measure or Not to Measure................................... 157

Chapter 18 – Creating Reports 167

Chapter 19 – Thrive 177

Chapter 20 – Pulling It All Together 185

Chapter 21 – Talent Planning... 195

Chapter 22 – Leadership Selection Dos and Don'ts.......................... 203

Chapter 23 – What Do Allies Have to Do With It? 211

Chapter 24 – Expanding an ERG through Local Chapters 221

Chapter 25 – Leading Employee Groups: The Good, The Bad and The How 231

Chapter 26 – When You Need to Take Charge 237

Chapter 27 – Leading and Inspiring 243

Chapter 28 – Following My Own Advice.. 255

Acknowledgments 257

Introduction

Initially, I wanted to title my book – *My Day Job vs. My Gay Job: How to Use ERGs to Create Inclusive Space at Work.* Let me explain why.

I led an LGBTQ+ Employee Resource Group (ERG) for more than seven years. Over time, I began to refer to my job as my "day job" (for which I was paid) and my "gay job" (where my passions lie, done on a volunteer basis). During my tenure in various leadership roles in this ERG, I learned a lot. One of the key things I learned is the importance of balancing your paid job priorities with your non-paid job priorities.

I found my gay job much more fulfilling than my paid job and saw real and tangible impacts I was able to create through my ERG role. I started things in my volunteer role that I could use in my paid job, and vice versa.

3

The impact of my work and my ERG team's work significantly influenced people's lives both inside and outside the office. Some of the most fulfilling results were the stories of how something I did in my ERG role had a direct impact on someone feeling it was safe to bring their whole self to work. It is hard to describe the emotions you feel upon learning how someone finally felt safe to be *out at work* based on the initiatives that you led. I received an email from a colleague who had been struggling to come out to their team. He had planned to come out on a Friday but had lost his nerve before arriving at work. After arriving at work, he read an article about the launch of the company's Ally Program and came out to his team that afternoon.

Balancing your paid job with your ERG role is not for the faint of heart. It can be exhilarating, and it can be some of the hardest and thankless work you will ever do. Then again, if it were easy, everyone would want to do it.

In the end, with encouragement from my friend, Alyssa Dver, I decided I didn't want an ERG leader to by-pass this book because the title didn't accurately reflect the content – which explains why you are now holding in your hands,

The ERG Handbook: Everything You Wanted to Know About
Employee Resource Groups but Didn't Know Who to Ask.

This book's basis is everything I learned while balancing a paid job and an ERG job and finding success and satisfaction in both. I know first-hand being an ERG leader can be challenging: It is even harder when you don't have the resources or tools you need to work effectively and efficiently. Let's be honest: Sometimes, you just want someone to tell you what to do. This book intends to help ERG leaders at all levels of an organization, so they don't have to reinvent the wheel when taking on a new position.

As an ERG leader, I want you to remember not to take yourself too seriously. ERG work is about passion, and I can say for sure that the opportunity to have my ERG job was one of the reasons I remained loyal to and a part of corporate America for most of my career.

Creating more inclusive spaces at work is becoming more and more important, and I believe that ERGs are the key to making that a reality. So, I will say it again – ERG work is not for the faint of heart, but if I had a choice, I would do it again and again and again.

How This Book Is Structured

I wrote this book and the *ERG Handbook Companion Workbook* to help ERG leaders and those passionate about the work of ERGs. Through my own ERG leadership journey, I learned a lot and have heard from many others about their leadership roles' ups and downs. As Vice-Chair of the Employee Resource Group Leadership Alliance (ELA), I also regularly hear from ERG leaders asking for specific help and guidance.

ERG Roadmap

This book is set-up to serve as an ERG roadmap based on the *Inclusive Space™ ERG Progression Model* of Launch, Grow and Thrive. This model is essential to maintain focus on where you are in your ERG journey and keep an eye on the future.

The roadmap begins by setting a foundation in terminology, introducing both the *ERG Progression Model* and the pillars or focus areas most ERGs support. After that, the roadmap takes you through each level of the *ERG Progression Model* with a chapter dedicated to the primary areas you should focus on during each phase. For example, the Grow Phase is focused on budgeting/funding, communicating, programming, and measuring - there are chapters on each of these topics. The *ERG Handbook Companion Workbook* is filled with templates, worksheets, tools, and toolkits referenced in the book. It is not enough to just read about how to do something; I want to equip you to *go out and do it*. The last several chapters talk specifically about ERG leadership and the unique set of leadership skills needed to balance the paid job and the non-paid passion job.

You Can Do This

Whether you are launching a new ERG or leading an established one, I designed this book and the ERG Handbook Companion Workbook for you. Doing something you are passionate about and not paid for should be easier, so your focus can be on essential things like leading others and working together to create an impact.

My journey has been incredible in so many ways and writing this book has been a labor of love. I hope you find this book, along with the ERG Handbook Companion Workbook, valuable and that it empowers you and those you serve to go out and make your workplaces and world more inclusive spaces.

Part I.

Before You

Launch

Chapter 1 – What I Know

Over the years, I have heard from many Employee Resource Group (ERG) leaders seeking answers to their ERG questions. Each is trying to figure out how to build a better ERG mousetrap or just build a decent one and have no clue how to start. The request I hear most often is, "can someone just tell me what to do, give me the tools, consult with us to help us start this, take it to the next level?" I can help you with each of these. I am going to share with you what I have seen, lived through, and learned.

I worked my way up through ERG leadership, and I think this is the very best way to do it. By moving through the process of development and leadership growth, you have a few things working in your favor. First, people know you, and they know your work and feel you have earned the position. Although I often tell my children, "don't worry about what other people think," sometimes it works better when we do. I have found that when assuming leadership roles, particularly when you are leading volunteers, having people feel that you earned it makes it easier to instill trust. People who trust you are much more likely to listen and to buy into your vision.

My national ERG leadership journey started with being asked to be the communication lead for an LGBTQ+ ERG. During my tenure in this role, I met a variety of people and got to know the folks focusing on communications at the chapter level.

Connecting to and understanding what is happening at the chapter level or local level is critical.

Knowing what the issues are with chapter level communications and knowing what problems are being addressed at the national level, you'll help build a bridge of communication between the national ERG and local chapters. My bridge-building skills resulted in a communication toolkit for Bank of America LGBT Pride chapters that we later tailored for all its ERGs. The toolkit gave people, regardless of communication experience, the tools they needed to get the job done (as volunteers) and gave them confidence that they were doing so in a professional and brand-compliant manner.

This toolkit allowed me to become the go-to person for that ERG's communications and fostered relationships and trust that encouraged people to ask permission instead of forgiveness.

My next role was the Southeast Regional LGBTQ+ ERG leader, where I was responsible for seven chapters in my region. I met regularly with the other three regional leaders and the national leaders to ensure we were all in sync and that we were addressing concerns and issues at the chapter level. This time together also allowed us to share all the great things our chapters were doing. It was and still is a great model.

By the time I become the ERG national co-lead, I had already established myself as a leader, teammate, and someone who cared. My co-lead came from leading the Northeast region. We became the dynamic duo; she was the first woman to co-lead the LGBTQ+ ERG, and I was the first ally to co-lead.

In addition to all my Bank of America experiences, I now have a network full of creative ERG people who have shared and will continue to share their experiences and stories with me. I would have never met these incredible people if I hadn't said **yes** to becoming an ERG leader.

Chapter 2 – What's in a Name?

Let's get the formal definitions out of the way first. Wikipedia defines **Employee Resource Groups** (ERGs) and **Employee Networks** (ENs) as voluntary, **employee**-led **groups** that foster a diverse, inclusive workplace aligned with organizational mission, values, goals, business practices, and objectives. Other benefits include the development of future leaders, increased **employee** engagement, and expanded marketplace reach.

Affinity groups (AGs) are groups of people having a common interest or goal or acting together for a specific purpose (as for a chartered tour).

Business Resource Groups (BRGs) are "about," not "for" a particular employee or customer demographic, with optimal membership consisting of a broad, diverse representation of a company. Successful **BRGs** embrace group knowledge and connect it to the business plan.

Formal definitions are great, but what do these really mean in practical application? To answer this question, let's look at how that might work in real life.

You are new to a company, and you're a member of the LGBTQ community. You would like to find a group with other members of your community, but you can't think of the name of those types of groups, so you do a Google search, and you find:

- Employee Resource Groups
- Affinity Groups
- Business Resource Groups

What do all these mean, and are they different? If they are different, then how? Well, the answer is that many people, including diversity & inclusion practitioners, use some of the terms interchangeably. Understandably, there can be confusion around their meaning. Having conducted my own research during my seven years in ERG leadership, allow me to clarify these terms for you.

Affinity Groups

Affinity Groups (AGs) were started in the U.S. in the 1960s, mostly as white caucuses and caucuses of color. These caucuses evolved into affinity groups. Affinity groups have since become ERGs and BRGs.

Affinity Groups are most often informal in structure, and leaders are usually self-appointed. These groups are often self-funded and don't have a formal executive sponsor role, although an executive might align themselves to the groups and provide guidance. The focus of AGs is usually more social. Think of AGs as a steppingstone to the creation or evolution of an Employee Resource Group.

Employee Resource Groups

Employee Resource Groups (ERGs) are much more structured and formalized than AGs. Think of ERGs as grown-up AGs. ERGs are supported by Human Resources (HR), the Diversity & Inclusion (D&I) Office, and Executive Leadership. This support ensures ERGs are more integrated into the organization and aligned to the company and its values. ERGs usually have a formalized structure, which includes executive sponsors and an ERG leadership team. ERGs leaders are typically elected or appointed, and they report to the group's executive sponsors. There is almost always some level of oversight from the D&I office.

As an ERG matures, it will develop chapters, and as the number of chapters increases, regional leaders can be added to the ERG leadership structure. The focus of the ERG aligns with the name Employee Resource Group. Their focus is on employees, developing emerging leaders, creating mentor relationships, developing programming that creates a more inclusive workplace, and by doing so, reducing turnover.

Some smaller organizations will never need to expand by creating chapters. You can still grow and mature and even contribute to business goals. Small can be mighty!

Business Resource Groups or BRGs

Sometimes BRGs are referred to as grown-up ERGs. This logic assumes that BRGs are somehow better than ERGs, and I disagree with this assessment. I think both groups have important functions, and there are places for both in an organization. I agree that many BRGs can grow out of, or branch off from, a well-run ERG. However, I don't entirely agree with an ERG model becoming a BRG model. BRGs' focus is on business development and driven by business strategies. With this business focus, the employee is no longer front and center.

For the best of both worlds, I prefer a well-run and mature ERG that creates a BRG team or committee aligned to business development. This model allows the employees to remain front and center while allowing a strong focus on the business that aligns with the demographic represented. For example, you can have an ERG and use the leadership and members to provide valuable feedback regarding product development and marketing to the demographic represented by the ERG.

To keep things simple, when I refer to ERGs in this book, I am using it as an umbrella term for ERGs and AGs. BRGs are a different kind of animal, so I will use the term BRG when referring to that specific group type.

Many companies choose to call their ERG-type groups names that better fit their culture. Examples: Colleague Resource Groups, Affinity Networks, Employee Networks, Colleague Networks, etc. Changing the name to better match the company culture is always the right decision.

Now that you understand what these groups are, the next question is: Why are these groups important?

Chapter 3 – Why Are ERGs Important?

Employee Resource Groups (ERGs) in different forms have been around for more than 30 years but are now more critical than ever to attract and retain diverse talent. They have re-emerged as a necessary, expected perk and voice for employees yearning for a deeper sense of belonging by accessing professional development, mentorship, and valuable connections. ERGs are invaluable in making diversity and inclusion (D&I) not just something you do, but who you are as a company.

The following are great things to include in your business case for launching an ERG.

Research shows that if employees can bring their whole selves to work, they are:

- More productive
- Strong brand ambassadors
- More involved in the communities they serve
- Less likely to leave

Increasing Productivity

ERGs create opportunities for people to use skills and support something they are passionate about outside of their paid job scope. This creates a space not only ripe for innovation but in an ERG, employees can foster interest and learn and expand skillsets. Many of these newly acquired skills translate to higher performance in their paid jobs.

Everyone wants to feel a sense of belonging. Companies that support ERGs empower employees to help create a sense of belonging for themselves and others. Happy employees are more productive employees.

Brand Ambassadors

My work in ERGs made me a stronger brand ambassador for my company. I was proud to talk about my company's work supporting diversity and inclusion and demonstrating how they walked the talk. I was proud to share the work we were doing in the ERG when interacting with other people personally or professionally, such as at a conference. I was eager to present my expertise and experience, and this enthusiasm inspired other ERG leaders both in and outside the bank."

Time and time again, I saw this with people involved in ERG work, not just with leadership but also with members. Social media is another way to see employees engage positively with the company's brand. I have seen employees spread the word about how proud they are to work for companies that value and promote diversity and inclusion.

More Involved in the Community

By sponsoring events and creating volunteer opportunities, ERGs give members various ways to be more involved in their communities and provide a conduit to extend that sense of belonging outside the workplace. It is an opportunity for potential customers/clients and potential employees to see the company and brand in a positive light.

Employer of Choice

ERGs also offer opportunities to network and meet people across different roles, departments, and business lines. They provide a safe place to try new skills such as learning to lead, managing a team, and contributing innovative ideas. ERGs give employees opportunities to gain confidence and build experience in an area they have a passion for but differs from the skillset in their paid job. Once comfortable with these newly acquired skills, they are often applied in their paid job, making them an even more effective employee.

Studies show that ERGs can be valuable to onboard new employees. Starting a new job can be scary and stressful, especially for those in marginalized communities. Imagine for a moment being a new employee who is part of the LGBTQ+ community and finding out during your new employee orientation that your new company has a group that represents your community, including a strong network of allies. Or consider being a Black woman and finding out on your first day, there are groups supporting two of your intersections of diversity – a Working Women's ERG and a Black Professionals' ERG. Just knowing that support teams are available makes the first day jitters a little less burdensome because you know you are seen and welcomed for who you are, not just for the skills you bring to the table. On the flip side, imagine arriving in a new workplace, and you are the *only* person like you, with no community...the isolation can feel overwhelming.

My ERG experience created a strong sense of company loyalty and made me want to do more in my paid and non-paid ERG roles. It was an honor and privilege to be allowed the opportunity to be a part of something that I was passionate about and could make a positive impact on my workplace and my world.

Real-life Example: The moment Amanda joined a professional women's ERG

Amanda was a communications support partner for a male executive in a technology organization. Amanda was a professional with over 15 years of experience in her field. One day Amanda's manager forwarded an email he had received from this executive referencing an email he received from Amanda earlier that day. In a nutshell, the executive was asking if something was wrong with Amanda. He said her tone in the email raised some red flags for him. Mike, her manager, told Amanda that he had taken care of it and not to worry about it.

Amanda re-read the email to see what red flags this executive could possibly be talking about. Well, it didn't take her long to realize that there was nothing in her tone that was unprofessional or should have raised any red flags.

She did, however, recognize that it was her directness that had caused an issue. She also realized if the same email had come from one of her male colleagues, there would have never been an issue as we're biased to expect men to be direct. In contrast, women are expected to be conciliatory in their communications.

Amanda called Mike and explained to him that this was unacceptable.

Mike blew it off as not a big deal – telling Amanda, "You know how he is."

Amanda hung up with Mike. She joined the Professional Women's ERG right then and there.

What do you think spurred Amanda to join the Professional Women's ERG?

She knew that it was vital for her to be herself: a strong, competent, and direct woman. Amanda also needed to feel a sense of belonging and understanding.

Amanda felt it was important for her manager to understand the impact this exchange had on her and for him to be in her corner: unfortunately, that was not the case. Amanda knew that by joining the Women's ERG, she would be surrounded by other women who could help counsel her through the experience and develop strategies to re-engage with her manager. The ERG would also be the best place to use her experiences to help other women cultivate and educate male allies.

Chapter 4 – Let's Get Structured

There are many ways to structure ERGs, and there is no right or wrong way. ERG structures vary by organization, but a general rule is to keep these groups' structures simple and straight-forward, focusing on employees.

A new ERG will have one group, which I refer to as the National ERG. The ERG leaders will usually report to the D&I Office and have a dotted line type of reporting relationship with their executive sponsors.

To help think through how you might want to structure your ERG, let's look at examples representing three different types of organization – (Corporate) Bank of America, (Academic) Yale University, and (Municipality) City of Dallas.

Corporate: Bank of America's Employee Networks

The Global Diversity & Inclusion Council and a group of executive sponsors across the organization provide oversight to the bank's 11 Employee Networks (ENs). ENs are focused on helping the company grow stronger by providing teammates with the opportunity to connect, develop leadership skills, build strong ties with the communities they serve, and bring lasting value to business strategies.

Each EN has several executive sponsors and several co-chairs. The co-chairs lead a leadership team with sub-teams for business support, communications, events, membership, and programming. Leadership teams can create additional sub-teams based on their specific needs.

The EN co-chairs each serve an average of three years, which are staggered. To ensure a smooth leadership transition, an incoming co-chair comes aboard three to six months before an outgoing co-chair rolls off.

Two EN managers in the Global D&I Organization facilitate regular meetings for all EN leaders, support technology, and provide enterprise connectivity. These meetings allow EN leaders to share ideas, best practices, and provide opportunities to collaborate.

EN chapters have a similar structure to the national EN. ENs with large numbers of chapters have regional leaders who meet with and support chapter co-chairs in their regions. The regional leaders are members of the EN leadership team.

In addition to executive sponsors, there are Executive Councils, and Line of Business Councils aligned to the same diversity characteristics as several ENs.

Academic: Yale University's Affinity Groups

Yale University has eight affinity groups:

- Yale African American Affinity Group (2005),
- Yale Latino Networking Group (2005),
- Asian Network at Yale (2005), LGBTQ Affinity Group (2008),

- Working Women's Network (2013),
- Yale Veterans Network (2014),
- Future Leaders of Yale (2014), and
- DiversAbility at Yale (2016).

The Office of Diversity & Inclusion has operational and fiscal oversight of each affinity group.

Yale University is committed to creating an inclusive environment and respectful workplace culture for all staff members. It understands that affinity groups serve as a significant driver for recruiting and retaining minority staff members. The University knows the value that each group contributes to making Yale a recognized leader in diversity.

Structure of Yale's Affinity Groups

Each affinity group:

- Is assigned a senior level executive sponsor, Staffing Liaison, and Yale Police Department Liaison
- Has two co-chairs that lead a steering committee comprised of at least four sub-committees:
    o Communications and marketing
    o Programming and events
    o Career/professional development
    o Membership and community outreach

Some of the affinity groups have created additional sub-committees that focus on advocacy, book club, health and wellness, recognition, mentorship, family network, and social justice.

The steering committee members are the main planning body and attend monthly meetings.

The co-chairs lead for two-year terms that are staggered, so every year, a new co-chair is onboarded. Half of the affinity groups use a co-chair-elect model, allowing someone interested in the leadership role to shadow for six months to a year. The affinity groups are open to staff, post-docs, and faculty.

Municipality: City of Dallas' Employee Resource Groups

The City of Dallas has six ERGs. Five of them are active. Funding for The City of Dallas' ERGs is through membership dues, which are payroll deducted.

- Associations of Asian American City Employees (1998)
- Black Employees Support Team (1986)
- FUEL - Focus. Unite. Engage. Lead. (2018) *

- Hispanic Association of City Employees for Results (1990)
- LGBT Employee Association of Dallas (2015)
- Veterans ERG (2018)

Each ERG has an executive sponsor at the Assistant Director, Director, or Assistant City Manager level. The Human Resources Diversity Manager serves as the ERG Advisor to all ERGs. Membership is open to any City of Dallas employee and retirees, but retirees cannot hold an elected office. Each ERG has allies as members, and allies are eligible to hold an elected office.

The following roles are elected:

- President
- Vice President
- 1st VP
- Secretary
- Asst. Secretary / Recording Secretary
- Treasurer
- Assistant Treasurer
- Parliamentarian / Sergeant at Arms

The Program Chair is appointed or may volunteer.

Each officer serves a two-year term. At the end of each year, the outgoing President helps with the transition. Outgoing officers have a transition meeting with the incoming officers, where they onboard new officers and begin the transition of files and documentation.

As you can see, some organizations use the term leadership team; others use board; some have an executive council or an advisory board, while others use the words committee or team or workstream. If your ERG terminology is unclear, it can confuse volunteer leaders and make role clarity difficult. While your leadership team's structure may evolve from year to year as aligned with your ERG's priorities, it's essential to have some defined organizational structure.

Chapter 5 – The Inclusive Space™ ERG Progression Model

An ERG Progression Model should provide a framework to ensure each ERG's consistency and accountability without diminishing the uniqueness of the dimension represented. There are a few ERG Progression Models out there. Some models are complex, and others are very strategic. I based *The Inclusive Space™ (IS) ERG Progression Model* on my experience and the need for things to be simple and more focused on getting things done rather than on academic language and 50,000 feet of strategies. Those models are not wrong, and the Inclusive Space™ model can work with those other models. I designed my model to be more of the *Git Her Done* model.

The Inclusive Space™ Progression Model has three stages: Launch, Grow, and Thrive. (I tried to come up with a cool acronym for this model but let's just stick to Launch, Grow, and Thrive.)

The important word here is "model." The IS Progression Model is not the end all be all, but a guide. An ERG Progression Model helps ERG's maintain their focus and avoid trying to do everything. You should also know moving in between stages or having one foot in one phase, and the other foot in another phase is just fine. Movement between these stages is normal and healthy, especially when you change leadership or start launching chapters. This movement is important to recognize, regardless of where you and your team are in your ERG journey.

> *The Inclusive Space ERG Progression Model works whether you are creating a new ERG, starting a chapter in an existing ERG, or considering new ideas for a tenured ERG.*

This progression model is simple and straight-forward. It may not be as high level and philosophical as some other models you may have seen, but there is a method to my madness. This model is usable and reusable, not something you use once and put on a shelf to gather dust.

> *This progression model works well with small, medium, and large organizations.*

Pre-Launch and Launch

Before you launch your ERG or chapter, you will be in what I call the Pre-Launch Phase. If this suggests a rocket launch – good because I want you to think of it that way. What you do before you launch will determine how quickly you can move into the Grow Phase. I am not saying that you need to hurry to the Grow Phase – please don't rush to get there. If you rush, you are going to be calling out – "Houston, we have a problem." (I live in Houston, so I love this reference.) Building a strong foundation will support your ERG's sustainability, and foundations take time to set. What do you need to do in the Pre-Launch Phase?

There are several Pre-Launch items you need to address to ensure your launch is successful. In this phase, you will focus on building your business case, creating your mission and vision statements, drafting your charter, and figuring out an ERG governance model.

What do you do during the Launch Phase? You launch your ERG, of course. You will also focus on building relationships with your executive sponsors and establishing leadership meeting routines. I will talk more about all these points and more in **Preparing to Launch** and **Launch**.

Grow

This phase is the biggest and busiest of the three phases because, well... you're growing. The Grow Phase can also be a lot of fun. In the Inclusive Space™ model, the Grow Phase is where you will focus on action items such as communications, funding, programming, and so much more. Never fear; I will take you through the Grow Phase with plenty of advice and, of course, suggested templates and worksheets.

Thrive

I *love* this phase. When an ERG is thriving, there should be room for an abundance of creativity and innovation to evoke broader and more powerful impacts. Thrive can be scary too. With greater visibility comes greater responsibility. As an ERG leader in this phase, you will most likely be in situations requiring you to use your visibility and your role to push the envelope a bit. You will create routines for multi-year planning, talent planning, and ramping up metrics and reporting during Thrive.

To help you be successful, all the worksheets, templates, and tools discussed during each phase are available in the ERG Handbook Companion Workbook and online.

Chapter 6 – The Pillars

Most ERGs will be required to align their work to several areas of focus or pillars. Pillars are essential because they demonstrate how the ERG aligns and supports the company's culture and values. Terminology doesn't matter if everyone is clear on their function. For this discussion, I will refer to these as pillars.

Most companies expect ERGs to support some or all five pillars below:

Community

This is a pillar that the ERG has a lot of control over. What can the members do within the communities you serve? Those within the communities need to see themselves valued and respected by the company and employees. Many of today's customers want to see companies that are both diverse and inclusive. ERGs are a powerful way to demonstrate that.

External Recruiting

ERGs can be powerful recruiting tools that can make your company stand out to future employees. Seeing a company that walks the talk when it comes to D&I can make your company rise above its competitors. Helping recruiters understand how to connect with and successfully hire new employees from your communities is invaluable.

Workplace Environment / Culture

How does your ERG make your company's culture/work environment the best place to be? ERGs should own this pillar. Through programming and education, your ERG can reinforce your company's culture, provide your members' perspectives and, in some cases, even shape the culture in ways that improve the environment for all employees. That is powerful!

Professional Development

Your executive sponsors, national leaders, human resources partners, and Diversity & Inclusion teams should all ensure that ERG leaders are a focus of professional development. Now let me be clear, I am NOT saying that ERGs have no skin in this pillar...you do! We must own our professional development, but ERGs can influence those listed above to support leaders' professional development. ERGs can also work with those partners listed above to help create a targeted professional development plan for ERG members. Some ideas for professional development initiatives are leadership training, confidence workshops, ERG specific leader training (Inclusive Space™ can help here.), mentoring programs, etc.

Business Strategy

How does your ERG support the business? For example, a company reached out to an ERG for information and support when questions arose about how the said company supported its LGBTQ+ employees and how it engaged in LGBTQ+ advocacy externally. ERGs can also be a great resource/sounding board for developing new products or getting the voice of certain customer community segments.

> *As an ERG, you are not wholly responsible for each of the pillars. A well-functioning ERG should own Workplace and Community and be a support partner for Recruitment and Business Strategy; ERG leaders should be both a support partner and consumer of Professional Development.*

Make sure to align your ERG's pillars with your company's culture. If you are new in the ERG space, your HR department will be a great resource to align your ERG's mission and purpose to your company's culture and the pillars you should support.

Aligning Activities to the Five Pillars

Community

Activities that support this pillar can vary widely and may include supporting a charity that aligns with the community the ERG represents, supporting social issues like homelessness, hunger, immigration, aligning volunteers with schools, coat drives, food drives, walking or building a float for a parade, festivals and so on. An excellent way to determine which activities your ERG wants to be involved in is to ask your members about their involvement with other community groups/activities and what people's interests and passions are.

External Recruiting

For some ERGs, especially new ones, this is harder to do. The best way to determine how you can help is to talk to recruiters at your company and ask where you might assist. Members of your ERG might ask to attend a conference to run a booth or attend events for colleges and universities where your company recruits. If you know of members who have connections to and interest in recruiting, don't be afraid to offer Human Resources help.

Workplace Environment / Culture

Activities in this pillar are where your ERG can shine and have a tremendous impact. Internal initiatives during diversity months are excellent ways to showcase your ERG, to educate others about the importance of inclusion, and how those interested can become allies. Two examples of this type of collaboration are the LGBTQ+ ERG partnering with the Black Professional ERG to screen the movie *Brother Outsider* during Pride month or the Veteran ERG partnership with the Disability ERG during Disability Month to raise money for companion services dogs. Improving your organization's environment and culture should be a primary focus of your ERG.

Professional Development

This pillar may include development for members and your ERG leaders and provide opportunities to collaborate across ERGs. Start by finding out if your company offers any professional development training. From there, you could schedule a webinar for members to attend. If your company has online learning, you could create a project team whose goal would be to set-up several professional development learning plans and make those available to members. Both options should require little or no budget. Another option is to bring in a speaker. Hiring a speaker would require funding, but it could be more reasonable if two or more ERGs split the funding. Mentors, current or past executives sponsor, or others passionate about diversity and inclusion can help provide professional development for ERG leaders.

Business Strategy

BRGs by their name and function should already be doing this; however, this can be tougher for ERGs since their focus is on the employees and not specifically on the business. I remember my co-chair and I struggling with this pillar, as did our predecessors. We came up with what I think is a great solution. Former executive sponsors for both the national ERG and chapters wanted to help, so we formed a team of these executives and let them take the ball and run with it. This model allowed us to maintain our ERG focus within our membership and still be able to support and have an impact on the business. Again, when we did this, we were a mature ERG, and we could recruit the resources to make this happen.

In the next chapter, we are going to pull this all together with the ERG progression model. Where are you in your ERG journey? Which pillars should you be supporting? Those answers are coming up next.

Chapter 7 – Progression Model, Pillars, and Activities

The final step in the progression model process is to create a routine for aligning and evaluating the ERG's pillars and activities with the progression model's current stage. Why is this important? By aligning to the progression model and the pillars, ERGs can align their ERG's mission and vision and their company's core values. Understanding these connections will also help you tell your ERG story as you talk with business leaders, members, and other employees.

Before we go any further, this is only a guide, and the activities are only examples. You will probably have times when your ERG looks like it is between progression model phases. That is okay. Aligning progression models, pillars, and activities are more of an art than a science.

To help facilitate this exercise, the next few pages offer a completed example of the **Aligning Progression, Pillars and Activities Template**. This template uses the Inclusive Space™ progression model and the five pillar categories discussed in **Chapter 5**. If your company has different ERG pillars, feel free to change the categories to match those pillars.

The tables in the next few pages lay out how pillars might line up in each phase of the *Inclusive Space™ Progression Model*.

A version of this template is available in the *ERG Handbook Companion Workbook*. A link to the downloadable version is also available in the *ERG Handbook Companion Workbook*. Again, this template is a guide; feel free to customize it to best represent and support your ERG. Making this a routine process allows ERGs to showcase their work and the impact that work is creating,

Make this process a routine. My suggestion is to review and update every six months.

Launch Phase

Pillar	Recruiting	Professional Development
What are you doing?	ERG members participate in the company referral process (if available) ERG makes itself available to learn how to assist D&I recruiting	ERG leverages HR and D&I to learn about company based professional development training
Examples of activities	ERG educates members on the company referral process and how to participate; ERG leaders attend a webinar on the D&I recruiting process	ERG team launches a survey to capture members' professional development needs; Team creates a spreadsheet of available Professional Development ERG focused training opportunities.

Workplace Culture / Environment	Community Involvement	Business Strategy (BRG)
ERG communicates broadly about their ERG and begins membership recruitment efforts	ERG members volunteer for one community event	ERG members encourage teammates to join the group
ERG creates a method to track membership; ERG sends a quarterly membership newsletter	ERG members work at a food bank or Habitat for Humanity build	ERG members and leaders forward event invitations to colleagues and business partners; ERG leaders speak/present at business meetings to share the value of the ERG

Grow Phase

Pillar	Recruiting	Professional Development
What are you doing?	ERG builds partnerships with recruiting offices. ERG members assist in recruiting efforts.	ERGs partners across diverse demographics to create professional development programs/events focused on ERG leaders.
Examples of activities	ERG members provide input on a company-sponsored recruiting event; ERG members staff a booth at a diversity conference	ERGs launch Professional Development program specifically for ERG leaders

Grow Phase

Workplace Culture / Environment	Community Involvement	Business Strategy (BRG)
ERG collaborates with other ERGs, HR, and D&I to drive a culture of inclusion.	ERG develops strategic partnerships in the communities served.	ERG demonstrates a broad understanding of business acumen.
LGBTQ+ ERG and Black Professionals group host a courageous conversation on being Black and LGBTQ+	ERG chooses and supports one specific organization each year.	ERG team helps implement a strategy to support a product/service need aligning to the ERG's demographic.

Thrive Phase

Pillar	Recruiting	Professional Development
What are you doing?	ERG aligned to D&I recruiting efforts as a trusted advisor and supportive volunteers.	ERG demonstrates how ERG involvement impacts retention. ERG works to improve and influence the development of a diverse talent pipeline.
Examples of activities	Women in Tech ERG work with recruiting to interview candidates at a Women in Tech conference.	Hispanic Professionals ERG track metric that demonstrates improved retention and promotion rates due to ERG involvement.

Workplace Culture / Environment	Community Involvement	Business Strategy (BRG)
ERG is viewed as a consultant/advisor on trends and issues in the workplace impacting employees. ERG develops and launches initiatives that positively affect employees' engagement and satisfaction.	ERG grows partnerships with external organizations through volunteerism: ERG advises on D&I company funding to external organizations.	ERG demonstrates strong business acumen and alignment to business strategy - impacts to strategy aligned to the ERG's demographic.
Black Professionals ERG sought out to advise on the company's response to social justice events. LGBTQ+ ERG launches a week focused on education and allyship.	LGBTQ+ ERG aligns with LGBTQ+ senior citizens housing charity; Professional Women's ERG asked to choose and distribute grant money to a women's focused organization.	ERG brings forth ideas for new product development and partners with business through delivery.

Chapter 8 – Preparing to Launch

As the saying goes, before you run, you have to walk. And before you launch, you've got to complete pre-launch. This chapter is longer than most chapters in the book because everything you need to do in Pre-Launch is here.

First, gather a team of passionate people. This part should be easy and may have started before you formally decided to form an ERG. You can gather people from your professional/internal network, and then those people gather from theirs' and so on and so on. My recommendation is to have around 25 people willing to become members and help get the group up and running.

The number of members and your ERG size will vary based on your company's size. Multinational companies or organizations with thousands of employees may also have thousands of ERG members and potentially look for a larger organic interest than a smaller company. Conversely, a law firm employing 300 people might have much smaller ERGs but are still critical to those members' experience and connectivity.

Consider the makeup of your initial interest group; does it reflect a range of perspectives, or is it homogenous somehow? For instance, a disabilities-focused group might emerge from the Deaf and Hard-of-Hearing community. Still, the core group may not include people with vision impairments or teammates in wheelchairs. An Asian-focused group might arise from the Chinese community but not yet include members from other Asian cultures. Even if you don't have complete representation from all the future ERG members, try to appreciate their needs.

In the beginning, you will probably find that not everyone in your core group knows each other, but they do know they each share a common interest in the premise of the group. For an ERG to be successful, this core group needs to feel accepted, valued, and wanted. For most people, that means they want their true selves to be seen and valued, and their stories heard. At this point, I bet some of you are thinking, "Aimee, this is starting to sound like group therapy and not an ERG." Let me assure you that this is not group therapy, but it is critical to establish a common purpose and acceptance within your core group. If your core group doesn't feel bonded and accepted, how will you attract other potential members? Let's be honest; what everyone craves in life is to be seen and heard and BELONG! Creating space for the core team to get to know each other and to learn about each other's strengths and assets is essential. Getting to know each other can happen organically within the social time before a formal meeting starts, through group gathering activities and scheduled social events such as coffee or lunch.

Forming these core relationships becomes incredibly important when challenges arise. In the life of an ERG, you'll have leaders and sponsors come and go, capacity for individual engagement will change, and life will happen. There may be days where the passion work feels more like *work work*, or an idea or initiative isn't progressing as quickly as you'd hoped. Building a team of people who can lean on each other during difficult times is critical to your ERG's longevity and sustainability.

Before we take the next step, you need to answer an important question. Who is your team?

Getting Started

Once your core group is together, you start the work of getting things up and running. If your organization already has ERGs, find out who the ERG leaders are and schedule some time to talk with them. In the **ERG Handbook Companion Workbook**, the **Understanding Your Company's ERG Landscape Worksheet** is a framework for your conversation with these ERG leaders. Feel free to add your own questions to the worksheet. Conversations with people already doing this work can be invaluable in helping to successfully launch and run your ERG and help you avoid pitfalls. This information can also feed into developing your ERG business case.

Whether you are starting an AG or an ERG, most companies require that you create a business case and a charter to present to HR or D&I for sign-off. The goal is to get it presented and signed-off the first time so you don't have to revise and re-do the work.

The purpose of a business case is to gather and then present all the necessary information to make your case for starting an ERG, initiative, or project. As you begin developing your business case, consider the questions below to get your ERG off the ground. To make this process easier, use the ***Building Your Business Case Worksheet*** and the guidance below.

1. Who's on your team of passionate people?

You'll need between 20 and 25 team members. See the beginning of this chapter.

Make sure your core group demonstrates diversity.

---

2. Why is this ERG important to your company? What is the purpose of creating it?

An excellent way to outline your purpose is to have a couple of significant facts that will illustrate the need for this group. As an example, below are some possible fast facts for creating an LGBTQ+ group:

- One in five LGBTQ+ employees have experienced verbal bullying from colleagues and/or customers because of their sexual orientation within the last five years. *Source: www.stonewall.org*
- 13 percent of LGBTQ+ employees would not feel confident reporting homophobia bullying in the workplace. *Source: www.stonewall.org*
- 62 percent of Generation Y LGBTQ+ college graduates go back in the closet when they start their first job. *Source: www.stonewall.org*
- Closeted LGBTQ+ workers are 73 percent more likely to leave their jobs within three years versus those who are "out" at work. *Source: Harvard Business Review*

To help you with this part, start with the ***ERG/D&I Business Case Fast Facts Tool*** in the ***ERG Handbook Companion Workbook***. This tool is a compilation of different diversity facts and their sources to illustrate the need and importance of creating specific ERGs.

You can also gather data on what other companies are doing. If you start from scratch, finding out what other companies are doing in the ERG space can prove valuable when creating your business case. Reach out to other companies' D&I offices and ask if they will connect you with some of their ERG leaders. These leaders are a great way to get information and make valuable connections.

> *There are a growing number of D&I practitioner communities and ERG groups on LinkedIn; build your network while learning from others' experiences!*

> *A great organization to network with other ERG leaders is the ELA Leadership Alliance – www.ERGleadershipalliance.com*

3. **What are your company's values? Current culture?**

This info should be easy to find and is important to reference when creating your business case. Most companies include this information on their intranet and internet sites. Your D&I office is another useful resource.

> *The stronger you can connect the language and concepts to your company values and culture, the more likely your business case will be successful.*

4. **What are the vision and mission of the ERG?**

First, let's clarify what each of these statements is:

- **Vision statement:** Describes the ideal future of the ERG and what the group is trying to accomplish.
- **Mission statement:** Describes why the ERG exists and its function.

Creating mission and vision statements doesn't have to be difficult and should not be something so laborious you want to leave the room screaming.

Simpler statements are easier for ERG leaders and members to remember and repeat when sharing about the ERG with other people. For instance, your vision statement might be as straight-forward as, "Our ERG vision is to make this company the best place for Latinx people to work." Your mission could then be, "Our mission is to connect Latinx employees across the company with business leaders to provide insights and perspectives to take action and achieve our vision."

5. Describe the business opportunity.

List the reasons why this ERG is valuable for business reasons. For example, improved brand recognition, improved recruiting, not just in the diversity represented by your ERG but across all diversity groups, improved employee engagement, reduced attrition, etc.

It's essential to know what's important to your company! If you're pitching the idea of reduced attrition, but your company is okay with turnover and is more focused on productivity and engagement, you'll miss the mark. Departmental scorecards, business review documents, shareholder reports, and other business documents will help determine the most important angles from which to approach. Human Resources, the Diversity and Inclusion Office, or your executive sponsor could help you get this type of data.

6. **What resources can provide input into the business case?**

List the resources used to provide input into the business case. Include any high-level executives that are engaged and have provided guidance. Some input resources to consider are your executive sponsors, the D&I office, Human Resources, and any ERG specific external research.

7. **What is the scope?**

Break down what to complete in the Launch Phase and what will wait for another phase. In scope: Create the leadership team, delineate their roles and responsibilities, secure and onboard executive sponsor(s), and host ERG launch events (member sign-up; distribute member needs survey, and willingness to serve).

Out of scope might involve hosting more than one event or partnering with other ERGs. Rethink things that would be more appropriate to tackle in the Grow Phase instead of in Launch.

8. What's the risk of not doing it?

Statistics and cost benefits can illustrate the risk of not doing it, i.e., the cost of attrition due to a perceived unwelcoming, intolerant work environment or cost of attrition due to the community's perception of not doing the right thing or not having a focus on diversity and inclusion. Your HR office is your best source for the cost of attrition information. If you cannot get this type of data from HR, pull out the *ERG/D&I Business Case Fast Facts Tool* and see what fast facts align with the risk.

Make sure your business case clearly addresses the need for this ERG at your company and the value it will bring to employees and recruiting.

---

9. Benefits – Return on Investment (ROI)

Tie the business case back to the risk, turn it around and show the savings, the increase in employee morale, and the overall business opportunities and benefits other companies have seen because of having ERGs. ROI is

71

another topic where your connection to ERG leaders at other companies can be beneficial.

10. **How will creating an ERG benefit employees and support your company's values and culture? How will it positively impact the culture?**

You should be able to align the benefits to employees and the company's culture. When thinking about benefits, you can use information from questions 2, 4, 8, and 9 to help make your case. The fast facts you used in question 2 can help you in crafting the employees' benefits statement.

11. **What are other companies doing in the ERG space?**

Again, gather data regarding what other companies are doing in the ERG space, including but not limited to the focus of the ERG you want to start. Consider whether your executives (or those who will approve or decline your business case) are more interested in the efforts of competitors or other companies in the same industry, or if they may find value in the perspectives of a variety of other companies. This information will help target your outreach and research.

12. **Create a list of possible executive sponsors**

Executive sponsors should be well thought of and influential with current employees, leaders, and others outside the company. Your team of passionate people is a great resource to brainstorm and vet some names. If there are already established ERGs in your company, then D&I or HR can offer input and make additional suggestions.

An ideal sponsor is senior enough to remove potential roadblocks, help open doors for your ERG and influence their peers to engage and support your group; however, they must also be available to offer their strategic guidance, advice, and coaching. A sponsor in name only may help get your ERG launched, but you'll need a more engaged executive in the Grow and Thrive Phases.

13. **Roles and Responsibilities**

In the beginning, the ERG doesn't need a complex leadership structure. Still, it needs a basic design and simple leadership roles that include clear responsibilities/job descriptions. Mirroring existing ERGs is a useful way to get started, but if there's no group yet to model, focus on the key roles noted. Use the ***ERG Leadership Roles and Responsibilities Worksheet*** as a starting point. Some suggested initial roles are: Co-leader, Business Support leader, and Events Leader.

> *Some companies may look for a finance or budget leader in the initial team and communications and marketing.*

14. **How will your ERG be governed?**

If your company already has ERGs, then you will follow the same governance model. If not, there are several governance models to consider. I recommend co-chairs that report to a designee in D&I or HR and connect to the executive sponsor. With guidance from the executive sponsor(s), the ERG leadership team's role and function are to govern the ERG. Refer to **Chapter 4.**

15. **Terms of office**

Generally, a leadership term of office is one two-year team, and no more than two consecutive two-year terms.

> *Once established, your ERG will begin to stagger leadership succession so that leaders overlap to share knowledge, connections and keep long-term goals and initiatives in focus and on track.*

16. **What are your one-year goals?**

Using information from question #7, refine your goals to be accomplished in the ERG's first year. This information will show that you are thinking past Launch and into Growing the ERG. You don't have to give a lot of detail but outline what you hope to accomplish. Some possible goals could be successfully launching the ERG; growing ERG membership to *X number of members* within 12 months from the launch date; creating at least one partnership between the ERG and a community group.

If you're like many fledgling groups, you have a TON of ideas! Consider what you might realistically accomplish with your current volunteers and leadership team and select the most impactful ideas. Other items can be added into a more comprehensive strategy document used by your leadership team in the Grow and Thrive phases; you won't lose the ideas, but you won't feel bogged down by more work than is manageable.

Building Your Business Case

Guess what? After completing the **Building Your Business Case Worksheet**, you will be ready to assemble your business case. As a reminder, when creating your business case, it's crucial to ensure you have well-developed ideas and concepts.

Like any other business case, provide the following necessary information:

- Proposal title and executive sponsor(s)
- Business opportunity
- Proposal input
- Benefits to employees, customers, clients, and share-holders
- In-scope/Out-of-scope

- Risk of not doing it

Use information from the worksheet as a guide in drafting your business case.

> You don't have to reinvent the wheel. Use what other ERGs have used and tailor it to your specific needs.

Once you have completed the *Building Your Business Case Worksheet* and put together your business case, you are ready to fill out your charter.

The Charter

To make this easy, there is an **ERG Charter Template** in the **ERG Handbook Companion Workbook**. With all the information you completed in the *Building Your Business Case Worksheet*, filling out your charter will be a breeze.

Applying to Establish Your ERG

To start an ERG, some companies require an application process. The process includes completing a simple application form then attaching your charter and your business case. If your company doesn't have an application template, you can use the **ERG Approval Request Template.** The application traditionally includes information you have already gathered for your business case, typically presented as:

- Name of the Employee Resource Group
- Name of the employee(s) organizing the ERG
- Group's purpose?
- Employee Resource Group's mission statement. This should be the same as in your ERG Charter.
- Provide three examples of how your group's mission and purpose will support the company's mission, values, and culture
- Attach your Charter. Please describe your leadership structure and how leaders are elected, terms, and communication to the membership
- Provide signatures of at least 25 employees who indicate they will join your Employee Resource Group

The steps to get an ERG up and running are simple and straight-forward. The key is to do your due diligence and not skip any steps.

Work closely with the D&I office or another ERG: An established ERG is a great place to start. They should provide you with sound advice on what to do and how to do it along with lessons learned and what not to do.

Part II.

Launch

Chapter 9 – Launch

Now you have finished everything needed to launch your ERG: you have done your homework, completed your business case, charter, and are ready to go. The Launch Phase sounds like it will be concise. You launch, and then you are onto the next phase, right? Well, not exactly. ERGs will remain in the launch phase *until they build a solid operating foundation.* Taking time to build a solid foundation is not a bad thing – it is a positive way to ensure that what you have created so far will continue to Grow and then Thrive.

First Things First

How do you launch your ERG to ensure you get the most bang for your buck? There are a few ways to launch an ERG. One way is to have a soft launch with your core group of leaders and members. This event should be social with a focus to equip this core team to become ERG ambassadors. Core team members can share a one-pager with attendees illustrating why this ERG is needed and the ERGs mission and vision statements,

With your core group of ambassadors, the next step could be a launch event open to everyone. This event could be an internal event like a virtual launch or a brown bag informational lunch. Be creative and use the collective brainpower of your core group ambassadors.

Some groups want to have a massive launch event or gala. Based on your company culture, this may be the right choice for your group. However, this can be a recipe for early burnout. If the new leadership team pours all of their energy into a single event, it might be several months before you're back on track with regular monthly member meetings or events.

If you choose this launch route, two words of advice:

1) Recruit enough hands-on-deck that the effort still feels fun and exciting, and;
2) Keep a handful of people focused on the next event AFTER launch. Smaller or less orchestrated events like lunch-and-learns or discussion groups are also good options. You want to have something to announce at your

big event! It is important to have a "what's next" message and event to share with the excited attendees.

Remember, it is okay that everything is not perfect when you launch. If you wait until everything is perfect, you will never launch!

Launching is a marathon, not a sprint. Half the fun and the rewards are taking time to create a design that you can manage. Get the right personnel to fill the most critical roles and then push the button for liftoff.

What Next?

Now that you have launched your ERG, there are areas to focus on to ensure you have a solid foundation before you can Grow and Thrive. You want an ERG that makes an impact.

Relationship Building

The relationships between leaders of the ERG and their executive sponsors are crucial. Good working relationships need to have a solid foundation, and one of the best ways to create that is by being clear and transparent about needs and expectations.

ERG leaders need to ask for what they need from their executive sponsor and for the executive sponsor to articulate what they will contribute to their role and what they expect from their ERG leaders.

To help get this relationship off on the right foot, there are two tools in **Chapter 10**, one for ERG leaders and one for executive sponsors.

Establish Meeting Routines

Set up meeting routines with your executive sponsors, your leadership team, and your ERG members. This sounds simple, but often people create matrices of meeting routines and complex agendas which don't accomplish anything. (Sounds like your paid job, doesn't it?) The beauty of working in the ERG space is you can cast off your day job meeting woes and create something you have always wanted.... sounds liberating, doesn't it? It can be liberating for your attendees as well. To ensure engagement and participation, be considerate of attendees' paid job obligations and create routines and agendas that make the best use of their time. The ***ERG Leadership Meeting Agenda Template*** is useful in setting up your regular leadership team meetings.

> *A shorter, more frequent meeting schedule may be more useful than a monthly hour-long meeting; this allows you to keep tasks and projects moving effectively.*

Establish Communications Routines

This is just like setting up meeting routines and agendas. All your leaders and members have day jobs; keeping this in mind will increase participation and engagement in the communication process. I like to use the KISS rule, **K**eep **I**t **S**imple **S**tupid (See **Chapter 14**). It is important to remember that as your ERG moves into Grow and then Thrive, you will need to revisit and enhance your communication strategy. A communication strategy is not a one-and-done deal. Your communication strategy should be a living, breathing document that is regularly reviewed and updated. Your communications during the Launch

Phase will not be the same as your communications in Grow, and they will be more robust in Thrive.

ERG Leadership Model

Most companies have an overall or general leadership model (versus an ERG-specific one) for their organization. ERG leadership roles are opportunities for professional development and growth, just like a day-job leadership role. To reflect this, I recommend creating a simple ERG leadership model with eight to ten competencies with a short description for each.

Check with D&I and HR before starting this exercise to see if your company has an ERG Leadership Model. If nothing is available, then representatives from all the company's ERGs should create a working team. This cross-ERG representation will ensure the resulting leadership model can be used regardless of ERG or leadership role type. To develop the ERG Leadership Model, the team should have the company's Leadership Model and use the **ERG Leader Capabilities Template**. The result will be an ERG Leadership Model that aligns with the company's Leadership Model.

Once drafted, the ERG Leadership Model will need to be reviewed and approved by ERG executive sponsors and someone in the D&I office, HR, or both. Including someone from HR and D&I on the working team can help secure final sign-off happens quickly.

How Do I Keep Up with All This Stuff?

By this time, you have completed several templates, worksheets, and, hopefully, an ERG Leadership Model. The logical next question is, how and where does an ERG keep up with this stuff? There is no way to balance your paid job and your non-paid passion job without some organization. There are lots of different ways to organize and maintain. One ERG I have worked with created some easy and free ways to keep things organized. The important thing is to find something that works for you and your ERG.

No individual ERG wants to spend precious ERG budget on business administration tasks, but that doesn't mean you can't get organized. For example, one ERG business support manager created an ERG SharePoint site. Within that site, she created several folders for things like:

- Tools

- Templates and worksheets
- Data
- Reporting
- Leadership team meeting minutes and agendas
- Executive sponsor meeting minutes and agendas
- Budget and funding
- Membership
- Member engagement
- Events
- Communications

This method helped keep everything together and limited access to only people in roles that needed access. When this ERG expanded into local chapters, a folder with similar sub-folders was set-up for each chapter to manage. This method works well if access is kept up to date, including removing access when people rotate out of roles or leave the company.

There are also a handful of software platforms available, designed specifically for ERGs. They include event management, email, budgeting support, and other management and marketing features helpful to ERGs. These may be cost-prohibitive for individual ERGs, but many companies are purchasing these platforms to manage their ERGs and empower the ERGs to manage themselves better.

Some companies choose to build their own ERG management platforms. In most cases, larger companies with technology departments can develop a platform to company specifications. If you are fortunate to have this tech support, this can be a great way to get the specific software support you need.

The earlier in the ERG journey you choose an organizational solution, the better off you will be.

Congratulations! You are on your way. I can tell you from experience that this journey will be some of the most challenging but most rewarding work you will ever do (and it can be a lot of fun, too!)

Chapter 10 – Welcome Aboard Executive Sponsors

Because of the word "executive" in executive sponsor, some people assume this role is more about oversight than a hands-on activity. I have known and worked with several executive sponsor types. Some were good, and some were awesome. So, what was the difference? Some of it was personality, but a big part of it is how they viewed their responsibilities as executive supporters. Good executive sponsors view their role as oversight and helping to remove roadblocks. The great ones do this AND have a passion for the ERG's mission and vision and are willing to help carry the load.

> *Your executive sponsor's assistant or business support manager (whoever runs their office and schedule) is someone to get to know immediately. They have the inside view of how their executive likes to interact with their team, the kinds of conversations and documents which impress and engage them, and pitfalls to avoid to ensure you're making a great impression with the new sponsor.*

What Can You Expect from Your Executive Sponsor?

Executive sponsors play an important role in your ERG.

Actively Participate

A sponsor in name only isn't an effective sponsor – they need to show up! Members might be excited or interested when the executive sponsor is in attendance but it shouldn't be such a rare sight that people are surprised to see them at ERG meetings or events. Members should be accustomed to seeing them engaging in activities and events.

Amplify the ERG / Network

Executive sponsors should be able to communicate the ERG's value to the company and for the business. Their peers and direct reports should hear them speak about it regularly, understand why they are serving as an executive sponsor, and why it is important to them.

Provide Financial Support

An executive sponsor helps the ERG financially, but those funds don't have to come out of their budget. The executive sponsor should brainstorm with ERG leaders regarding how to raise funds independently. Funding is an important part of this role. Also, executive sponsors need to review financial requests and support ERG leaders when making the ask.

Coach and Develop

Coaching and developing ERG leaders is an essential role of an executive sponsor. They must have a vested interest in the success of the ERG or chapter and the ERG leaders they are coaching and developing. ERG leaders need and

95

deserve an executive sponsor who is skilled in leadership development and coaching. Most successful leaders are not in this for themselves. They are involved because it aligns with their values, and they are passionate about the mission and vision of the ERG.

Remove Roadblocks

There will be times your executive sponsor will need to help you remove roadblocks. For example, sometimes politically charged issues arise in the workplace. When faced with a politically charged issue, it might be the time to make a call to your executive sponsor. They should coach you about going around, getting through, rethinking, or finding a different solution before they step in and remove a roadblock.

Have Your Back

It is important to cultivate a relationship with executive sponsors. They should be your first call when an issue arises that you are concerned about how it might reflect on you. My ERG co-lead and I always knew that no matter what, our executive sponsors had our backs. We referred to them as our air traffic controllers.

Onboarding Your Executive Sponsor

It seems that this task is something not many ERGs do well. I have been to many conferences over the years, and almost all of them have a workshop on **Executive Sponsors, Use Them or Lose Them**. Onboarding your executive sponsor is the first step in creating that working relationship I mentioned earlier. The best way to start most relationships is by setting clear expectations, and this is a great time to engage that executive assistant. You'll want to ask about the executive's preferences for meeting style, the kinds of documents and details that are particularly valued, and whether there is anyone else on the executive's team who likes or needs to be involved. This information will help you prepare for onboarding that ensures everyone is singing off the same hymnbook. In the **ERG Handbook Companion Workbook**, three worksheets should make it easy to establish a sound foundation to build upon and then move on to creating a solid working relationship between you and your executive sponsors.

The first worksheet is for the ERG leaders to complete: **ERG Leaders: What do you need from your executive sponsors?** The second is for the executive sponsor to complete: **ERG Executive Sponsors: What will you do, and what do you need from your ERG leaders?**

As an ERG leader, you need to know how your executive sponsor will promote the ERG, provide financial support, coach and develop, remove roadblocks, and provide air traffic control when needed. You need to let your executive sponsors know what you need from them. You also need them to be honest about what they need from and expect from you. My suggestion is to have each person complete their respective worksheet and then share it. After each of you has had time to review the worksheets, the next step is to complete the **ERG Executive Sponsor(s) Engagement Worksheet**. After completing this worksheet, schedule a meeting to talk through the information and come to an agreement about how you will work together.

> Don't skip over onboarding your executive sponsor. It is one of the most important relationships you will have as an ERG leader.

Scheduling a Meeting Routine

After you have laid a solid foundation for your working relationship with your executive sponsor, you need to schedule recurring meetings. At the beginning of your working relationship, you will need to meet more often, but as you become more established in your roles, you can probably move to monthly.

You should value the time spent with your executive sponsor. You have a limited amount of time to get through a lot of information. Therefore, be prepared so you can make the most of your time together. To make this easier, use the **Executive Sponsor Meeting Agenda Template** in the **ERG Handbook Companion Workbook.** This template helps get everyone focused, so you can make the most of your time together. The bottom line with executive sponsors: spending this time upfront will create a stable working relationship that will benefit you as an ERG leader and help the executive sponsor(s) maximize their ERG support.

> *Schedule several meetings in advance, likely quarterly, although more frequently if the sponsor is interested or specifically requests it. Scheduling in advance ensures time spent with your executive sponsor becomes an important routine.*

Part III.

Grow

Chapter 11 – Grow

Congratulations! You have launched your ERG! Now, we get to the fun stuff. The next phase in the *Inclusive Space*™ *ERG Progression Model* is Grow. The Grow Phase is full of helpful advice and strategies for you and your ERG. It is an exciting time as you and your leadership team begin to dig in and start creating an ERG that will impact your members' lives and your company's culture. Grow is a fun phase of ERG leadership, but there will be times where you have growing pains. Some important points to remember:

- You can't make everyone happy, so don't try.
- It is okay to make mistakes. Just make sure you learn from them and document issues so that future leaders don't repeat those mistakes.
- Even with all the passion from you and your leadership team, you CANNOT boil the ocean. I generally don't like to use the word can't, but, in this case, it is important! See bullet point one!
- The most useful tactic is to surround yourself with people who have skills that you don't or who are good at things

that you aren't. The next important tactic is to empower them to use the skills for which you recruited them.

Your ERG is in the Grow Phase; now what? During this phase, you will be:

- Recruiting your leaders and teams
- Working on a budget and funding
- Putting communication routines in place
- Planning programming
- Starting to use metrics

Recruiting Your Leaders and Teams

Now that the ERG has launched, the next step is to fill in the leadership team's positions. I have said it once, and I will say it again, the best leaders know their strengths and their not-strengths (I don't like using the phrase development needs or weakness). As a leader, you need to play to your strengths and recruit others whose strengths complement yours. Surrounding yourself with people with your same skillsets will not benefit you long-term, nor will surrounding yourself with *yes* people. The key to a successful leader is someone who recruits knowledgeable people with diverse skills and empowers them to use those strengths (For example, don't micromanage them.) People who are empowered and valued feel a sense of ownership and commitment to make whatever they are working on a success. **Chapter 12** will help walk you through this process and give you templates to help make it easier.

> *When you're recruiting help, consider including diverse perspectives, maybe someone who doesn't get it like you do. This difference in perspective can help you in recruiting not only additional help but also new members.*

Working on a Budget and Funding

How much or how little your ERG is funded will determine how much work will be required to create a budget and request funding. Even if your ERG is well-funded, you and your leadership team still need to create a budget. Next, the budget should be presented to your executive sponsor(s) and then to the Diversity & Inclusion Office or Human Resources. In **Chapter 13**, I give you tips and tools to make asking for money easier and hopefully more successful.

Putting Communication Routines in Place

Communications and the art of communicating is critical, regardless of where you are in the progression model. During the Grow Phase, the communication process should become routine. I recommend first selecting a communication team leader and team members to support that leader.

Because communication is vital to an ERG's success, I have written two chapters on the topic: **Chapter 14** and **Chapter 15.** When I was in ERG leadership, my paid job was in Corporate Communications, and my first ERG role was as a national communication leader. I know from experience how important creating reliable communication processes and routines is to the success of an ERG or chapter.

Programming

Another critical area for ERG success is programming. Programming (events, activities, initiatives, development programs) can determine many things, including:

- More current members becoming active members

- Successful new member recruitment
- Collaboration opportunities across multiple ERGs
- Level of ERG impacts in the workplace and the world

Chapter 16 should help ERGs hit the ground running in the Grow Phase. Remember, ERG leadership is an opportunity to think outside the box and maybe even create a new box. Programming is a great place to stretch an ERG's innovation muscle and activate your leaders' and members' ideas!

Metrics

The ever-elusive question, what to measure? **Chapter 17** will be your friend when it comes to this question. Measuring and reporting are important for ERGs to help demonstrate their value to the company, but it is essential to start small and work your way up when it comes to metrics. It is also essential to start early in the Grow Phase to make metrics and reporting a routine practice.

Don't Forget...

Meeting routines should be up and running. Talk to your leadership team and your executive sponsors and make sure things are working well. If you hit a bump or two in the road, that's okay: What's important is how you get over those bumps. The best way I have found to handle meeting routines is to ask people what is working for them and what is not. Once you know that, getting over the humps should be easy. After all, you can't fix something if you don't know it's broken.

Don't forget about your relationship with your executive sponsor(s). In **Chapter 10**, there were tips on working with your executive sponsor, including two worksheets – *ERG Leaders – What Do You Need from Your Executive Sponsor* and *Executive Sponsor – Your Role and What You Need from Your ERG Leaders*. This chapter and these tools can be used and reused to continue building and nurturing the relationship between ERG leader(s) and executive sponsor(s).

Growing Pains

During this phase, things can become a bit stormy as new voices are coming into the ERG. Don't worry; growing pains are the natural stage within Grow. There might come a time when the ERG loses members who decide the ERG's direction doesn't align with their goals - this is okay. There is a reason they're called growing pains. The focus of the ERG should be on the vision and goals and not on individual members.

And last, but certainly not least, ERGs should focus on checking in with members on their ERG satisfaction, priorities, and interests. The best and easiest way to do this is to survey members about what is working, what they would like to see in the future, and where they would be interested in getting involved.

Things are about to get fun and exciting, don't forget to enjoy the ride.

Chapter 12 – Recruiting Your 20 Percent

Recruiting and engaging volunteers is your most important role as a leader. Now that I have your attention, here is your first leadership tip:

> *When leading volunteers, especially volunteers who are as passionate as you are, everyone needs to focus on the ERG's mission and vision or, as I like to say, everyone should be "singing off the same hymnbook."*

Fact: 20 percent of volunteers do 80 percent of the work.

That is just how it is. If I find the miracle cure for this, I will write an addendum to this book and make it available to everyone free of charge.

The best places to go for volunteers are your current members, your network, and members of other ERGs and networks. I became involved in an ERG because I was asked by someone who knew that my skillset and passion could help develop the ERG he was leading. I stayed involved because I saw the difference it made in people's lives when they could be their authentic selves at work and, in turn, create a better work environment for all.

Finding Like-minded but Diverse Volunteers

If you are leading an ERG at a national level, you must know how to forge diverse working relationships and support other leaders who do the same. I got involved with Employee Resource Groups a bit by accident. I was at a Six Sigma training session in Dallas, Texas, with teammates from across the country. During that time, I met an awesome guy named James. We became fast friends and spent our downtime talking about our lives.

My life is an open book, and my support of the LGBTQ+ community as an ally is something that I share with folks. Why? Because it helps connect me to people who care about inclusion and equality. Sometimes it even allows me to educate people who are open to chatting. James knew that my day job was in corporate communications. During our time together, he discovered enough about me personally that he felt I would be a good fit for the LGBT Pride ERG communications lead role, so he made the volunteer ask of me. I took about a day to think about it, and when he called me back, I said **yes**.

I then had to begin recruiting team members to help me support national communications for the ERG.

Preparing to Ask

James and I knew that if you want people to volunteer, you need to actively recruit them. It is that simple. The hard part is how do you make the ask and get the **yes**. I have heard a lot of folks say that this is like selling yourself or your ERG. I disagree. It's about opening a door and inviting someone in. It begins with having a relationship with someone so that you know their interests and skillset.

It can be tricky to sell someone to do work on their own time and with no pay. But you will be surprised how many folks are willing to volunteer when you simply do one thing...ASK. "Seriously? All you have to do is ask?" In many cases, yes. However, making it simple means doing some work behind the scenes.

Let the Asking Begin

You are having an event and trying to figure out how to get people involved. You need help with a bunch of different tasks and no idea how you can get enough support to get it all done. The simple answer is to ask. I know what you are saying, "Aimee, I have asked, and I can't get the help I need!"

And my response is, "Maybe you aren't asking the right way."

Behind the Scenes

The easiest way to ask for support and get the **yes** is recruiting through relationships. The more you know about a person, the more you know what they can bring to the table. Your network is a great place to start. Start by making a list of all the people in your network who share your passion. This list will be a target-rich environment for volunteers. Then tap other ERG leaders for folks in their networks who might also share the same passion.

> *Instead of asking people to help with an overall event or project, ask them to help with one specific task.*

Real-life Example: John uses a specific ask to find a new volunteer

John was a member of the Church Council. The Church Council was dealing with a similar issue as an ERG: 20 percent of the volunteers doing 80 percent of the work. John was the Facilities team lead and was trying to figure out how to get more people involved.

The facilities team had a long list of responsibilities, and team members couldn't get everything done. So, John thought maybe if he broke down everything into smaller tasks, he could get more people involved. One job was regularly checking and changing the light bulbs throughout the building. It sounded simple, but it was essential.

John had seen Todd at church regularly, but Todd didn't seem to stick around after church or engage with others. John decided to approach Todd one day after church to chat. He told Todd that he would love for him to get involved and asked if he would take responsibility for checking and changing light bulbs. Todd said he would be more than willing to do that and was excited that John had asked.

After that, Todd became more engaged and volunteered for other tasks. All it took was someone reaching out and asking if Todd was willing to do one small thing.

So, you think you are ready to schedule lunch or coffee to make an ask? Well, guess what? The **ERG Leadership Assistance Request Worksheet** in the **ERG Handbook Companion Workbook** is here to help.

Questions you should consider before approaching a potential ERG leader or committee member:

- Is this person in my personal/professional network?
- What, specifically, am I asking this person to volunteer to do? To lead a team, be part of a team, lead a project, or do something one-off?
- Does this align with what they do in their day job?

- If not aligned to their day job, then what skills does it align to?
- What are they passionate about, and how is this role/project aligned to that passion?
- Job description – keep it short but hit the high points
- Volunteer time expected – How many hours a week or month, and for how long?
- Let them know why you think they would be a great fit and how excited you would be to have them on the team.
- Highlight the need for this exact person and how no one else will do.

Now go forth and make that ask (wooing should be included).

Thanks for Asking...

Now you have asked, here are the possible answers you might receive and the next steps to take.

"I would love to get involved!"

Congratulations, you got the **YES**! Now what? Use the checklist you prepared earlier and begin to get your **yes** onboarded. If their role is leading a team or committee with existing volunteers, schedule a quick meeting with the team to introduce everyone. If they are part of a team or committee, formally introduce them to the team leader and let them take it from there. (If you're not directly responsible for the person's onboarding to their new role, be sure that it's clear who is and that everyone is on the same page.) Forward or extend important meeting invitations or calendar placeholders and let them know their role in communicating with other team or committee leaders about the team's work. For example, will they be invited to a leadership team meeting where they or the team leader will provide regular updates on the initiative or project?

"I would love to get involved, but the time I have to volunteer is limited."

Ok, don't lose heart.

Ask what their realistic availability is and consider your team's needs – there may be a way for this volunteer to commit to doing something that requires less time but still matches their skill set and level of interest. If not, ask to keep them on a shortlist for future needs and check back in your next recruitment wave. This extra step shows them that you were genuinely interested in their participation, not looking for just anyone to do the work.

"No, I can't volunteer at this time."

For this, you say, "Thanks for considering it," and ask if you can check back with them in a month or two or during your next recruiting push. If you were recruiting for a national or global leadership team, be sure to offer to get them connected to any of your local ERG chapters or those of another ERG.

What now? Keep asking and keep following up. Some of those **no**s might become **yes**es later. You might be pleasantly surprised when someone comes back and offers to help, and you didn't even have to ask.

Chapter 13 – Show Me the Money

If your company already has ERGs, there should be some type of funding process in place. This process could be as simple as going out and sourcing your funding internally from leaders of departments, business units, or lines of business. Most companies, institutions, organizations, and government agencies have general funding for their ERGs, usually part of the D&I or HR budgets. Sometimes ERGs are funded through dues paid by members. Each funding model has its perks and its drawbacks.

My experience has been ERGs receive funding at the national level, and then those ERGs determine how to fund their chapters. Chapter funding is usually small, so chapters become resourceful in working with their executive sponsor to secure funding from leaders in their local area/market. Regardless of the amount of funding, it will never be enough to cover all the initiatives, special programming, and community events, which means there will be times when you will need to request funding for an event or program.

Asking for money is never easy, but when you are in a volunteer role leading an ERG, it can seem like you are 16 years old and asking for the keys to your parents' brand new car to go to the movies. You might hear lots of unsolicited advice from others about what you should or shouldn't do when making a funding request. In the grand scheme of things: you can't focus on the fear of asking. Instead, you focus on the passion for the ERG. If you are a natural salesperson, you might think you can skip this chapter. Well, you shouldn't. Remember, you are not selling a product or service that you will get a commission on. You are, however, selling your passion and your group.

> *Try to operate from a place of plenty and not from a place of scarcity. Be creative and thoughtful in deciding who is the best person to ask.*

Phrases like obtaining funding, asking for money, and dialing for dollars can make volunteer leaders shake in their boots. Well, stop shaking, and let's figure out how to do this.

Figuring Out Funding

Before you do any asking, do your homework. You can't expect to get the money you need without it. To prepare and create your funding business case, use the two worksheets in the **ERG Handbook Companion Workbook, ERG Funding Request – Part I,** and **ERG Funding Request – Part II**. Let's get started with some of the basics:

What ERG initiatives/events will require funding? - Events such as annual activities, festivals, parades, community service, and training events.

Know your membership - In which business units do your members work? Do you have members who make financial decisions for their business? Do your executive sponsors have access to dollars or donors?

123

Is there an opportunity to partner with other ERGs for an event? Funders like to see and fund events where more than one ERG is participating. Is there an opportunity to partner with ERGs within your company or even from other companies?

What are other ERGs doing? Can you come together and make a single ask?

Establish relationships - Who in your network may be a decision-maker or works closely with one? Invite decision-makers, marketing, employee engagement leads, and your cheerleaders to your ERG meetings. Never stop connecting and finding opportunities to demonstrate the value of the ERG.

Know your funding source - What have they funded in the past? What could they provide that would be a win-win for them and the ERG?

Before you make the ask:

- Prepare a budget
- Know your vendors
- Know the branding

Some points to address/answer in your request:

- Benefits to our employees
- Value adds for the company, business unit, or division
- List other ERGs, business units which are participating
- Outline any public exposure risks or opportunities (i.e., Social Media, Publicity)
- Align benefits of the event or activity with the company's core values
- List who will participate in this event
- List any others event sponsors

Leading an ERG requires creativity, and that includes getting things funded. For large events or initiatives, one supporter or sponsor may not be able to finance 100%, but you can use that to your advantage. Multiple decision-makers can get competitive, so never discount a little healthy competition. Don't forget about in-kind donations - printing fliers, providing event space outside the workplace, paying for snacks or a meal, and providing branded giveaways.

> *Business leaders are more likely to attend an event and encourage their teams to do the same when they've sponsored or contributed to the funding. Before pitching, consider what value you might offer back to the prospective event sponsor. For instance, you might say, "With your support, we're reserving ten spots on the front row for you and your team. Who would you like us to include in the invitations?" This approach assumes that they want to be involved and show up! It's a lot harder to turn that kind of offer down.*

Dialing for Dollars

My most significant dollar ask was for start-up funding for an LGBTQ+ Ally Program. Daniel, my co-lead, and I knew this would take some cash to do things the right way. We started by creating a business case. We knew if we could prove how the program could positively impact the company's bottom line, we would be well on our way to getting what we needed. The first step was arming ourselves with research. We found two statistics that we knew would get people's attention. We added other stats that would also get people's attention focused on *doing the right thing*, one of our company's core values. Next, we had to come up with a dollar amount and why we needed it. We determined at the very beginning that visibility and education would be the key to creating a best-in-class Ally Program.

After going through all the possible iterations, we realized this was going to be a huge ask. It was not unmanageable in the grand scheme of things for this C-Suite executive's budget, but this was a big one for an ERG initiative.

The Ask

Since our big ask was a program within a well-established ERG, it was essential to involve national leadership in the process. (I was in the unique position of co-leading the network and co-leading the start-up Ally Program, so it was easy to get myself onboard.) If your established team routines are working well, your ERG leaders will likely be aware of the funding need. Depending on the outcome's significance to the rest of the team, you might schedule a review or discussion before your pitch meeting with your executive sponsor.

> *For some teammates, an executive-level meeting is exciting, but for others, it can be stressful or unpleasant. Consider the important distinction - Who GETS to make the ask (privilege/reward) versus who HAS to make the ask (task/chore/punishment).*

Daniel and I had all the necessary buy-in, benefits, budget, and supporting data, so next was WHO *gets to make the ask?*

Fortunately, Daniel had a great rapport with the C-Suite executive, so he was tapped to make the ask. We scheduled a meeting with the executive, and together we presented our business case. The last slide was the *what we need from you* slide, which Daniel presented, and we got full funding. Getting everything you ask for will not be the outcome every time you ask, but I learned from this experience that you will never get a *no* or, more importantly, a big **YES** if you don't make the ask.

> *Your business case presentation should be well documented, organized, and in a concise format. Executives often have limited time to connect. Being clear and crisp with your ask and presentation will support a positive outcome.*

If you're managing a BRG, you may have a clear path to the funding source or partner within your own business, but the steps in this chapter can still help you prepare. Similarly, if you are running an affinity group that is self-funded or has a non-centralized funding model, you can also follow these steps.

Ask as a Group

What I mean by a group is not a group from the same ERG; instead, a group of ERGs asking together for funding. This approach works well for a group of ERG chapters, but it can certainly work for national ERGs.

Real-life Example: Patrick consolidates the budget requests from multiple chapters

A group of ERG chapter leaders in a large metropolitan city realized they were asking for funding from the same source throughout the year. This funding approach wasn't working well for the funding source nor for the ERG chapters.

Patrick, the leader of one of the chapters, had an idea. Instead of multiple ERGs making multiple requests, what if all the ERGs worked together to present one funding request for the year?

Patrick put together a working team with the other ERG chapter leaders. Together they developed a process and accompanying presentation to approach the funding source for funding requests for the entire year. This process was a win-win for everyone involved.

Due to its success, other ERG chapters viewed this as a best practice and began to adopt it as a part of their funding request model.

If you are thinking," Hey, this is a great idea, how do we get started?" I suggest each ERG or chapter complete the *ERG Funding Request Part I and II Worksheets* and then work as a team to create one business case for funding. Remember, once you get this process in place with the other ERGs, this will become a way to request funding just once a year for everyone, allowing each ERG to focus on their group's goals rather than individual funding goals.

Executive Sponsors as Funding Sources

Never discount your executive sponsor as a source for at least some funding. They might not be able to fund large ticket items, but they should be willing to identify other potential funding sources and assist you in preparing to ask.

The bottom line: Asking for and securing funding doesn't have to be scary or frustrating. Having an annual plan of your activities and events will limit the number of asks and ensure more **yes** responses that equal more dollars.

Chapter 14 –
Communicate,
Communicate,
Communicate

It sounds so simple, doesn't it? Communication should be simple, especially because we have so many ways to communicate. Well, here is the rub with communicating with ERG members: You are communicating with people at work who have lots of pressing paid job priorities. If you are communicating via email, you are a small blip in their inboxes. So how do you make sure that your members are opening and reading ERGs emails and newsletters? It's simple. I promise.

Real-life Example: Aimee creates a communications toolkit

As I mentioned in **Chapter 1**, my first ERG leadership role was as the national communication lead. Because my paid job was in communications, I didn't think this role would be a huge stretch for me, but I found in some ways it was.

Have you ever heard the phrase *herding cats*? Well, my first few months in this role felt more like *herding squirrels*. Not because people were uncooperative (well, a few were), but because everyone had their own ideas about how they were doing communications and the right way to do it.

To build engagement, I started with people who were already serving in a communication role either nationally or at the chapter level. Next, I pulled together a team of these volunteer communicators, and we started brainstorming on what their needs were and the needs of their respective chapters. Through significant time and effort, we came up with a communication toolkit for ERG chapter leaders.

This toolkit was so successful that the D&I Office asked me to partner with them to create a similar toolkit for all ERGs across the company. Several months later, we rolled out the ERG communication toolkit to all the company's ERGs.

Chapter 15 introduces templates and tools to create your own ERG communication toolkit.

Communication Tips and Tricks

Remember just a few key points when you are creating communications for an ERG – know your audience, keep it simple, be creative, you only have eight seconds, and subject lines are critical. Let's look at how you can do this as a volunteer.

Know Your Audience

To communicate effectively, you need to know your audience. What does that mean? Let's take a closer look by answering these questions:

- Who makes up your target audience? (Front-line employees, management, executive leadership, middle management, or a combination of each of these)
- What communication channels are available to each of your audience groups?
- What communication channels do these groups have in common?
- Is it necessary to communicate with any of these groups differently?

I want to emphasize again how important it is to start with your audience in mind. If you do that, then everything else will fall into place.

You Have Eight Seconds

Eight seconds is how long a bull rider has to stay on a bull, and it is also the amount of time to grab your readers' attention. According to a 2015 Microsoft Consumer Insights study, the average human attention span is eight seconds (a goldfish's attention span is nine seconds). I want you to set your phone timer for eight seconds to see how long you have to communicate or read the first sentence of this section, which will take you about eight seconds.

So, what can you do in eight seconds? If you keep it simple, you can effectively grab your reader's attention.

Keep It Simple

When I say keep it simple, I mean to be clear and brief. In communications, less really can be more. Using fewer words means more white space, and white space is a good thing. Your email is not an essay, and it is not conveying the nuclear codes. Use short sentences or bullet points, and group information together, such as date, time, location. Also, use simple, straightforward language.

> *Using a bunch of acronyms that people need to decipher will take focus away from the message.*

Be Creative

This role provides an opportunity for you and your communications volunteers to stretch your creative muscles while keeping within your company's brand standards for the ERG. It is also an opportunity to do some fun collaboration with other team members and members of the communications team.

Subject Lines Are Key

Having a subject line that grabs your attention might sound elementary to most of you, but it is critical. If you don't get someone's attention in the first eight seconds, then chances are they aren't going to open the email, much less read the message.

The name of this chapter says it all...**_Communicate, Communicate, Communicate_**. But don't assume overcommunication is your goal because it is not. Effectively communicating is such an important job that I recommend having a team that supports communications at the national level and then provides tools and guidance to your ERG chapters. The better you are at communicating your action plans, the more successful your ERG will be. Now, let's look at some tools to take your ERG's communications to the next level.

You don't have to say it all in the email. If your ERG has a website or wiki or another platform to connect or communicate with members, your email's goal is to get people out to your site, so they'll interact even more!

Chapter 15 – Tools for Your Communication Journey

This chapter is dedicated to tools to make ERG communications as easy as possible. The key is to start early, so your audience has plenty of time and multiple channels to receive information. All the tools discussed below are available in the **ERG Handbook Companion Workbook**.

Know Your Audience

Let's start with the **ERG Stakeholder Definition and Messaging Template**. This template will help you easily identify your target stakeholder/audience and determine the best way to communicate with them. Understanding who your audience is will help you craft relevant, motivating messages for your target audience. I recommend using this template to do audience analysis whenever your audience groups change. You can do one audience analysis to figure out how to communicate with your membership and maybe members of other ERGs. For a program launch or major initiative, like launching Ally Week or communicating to a broad audience during Women's History Month, you will need to add additional groups to your audience analysis. This way, you don't have to start from scratch every time. You can take your audience analysis for membership, add the new groups, and voila - you have a new complete audience analysis.

Below is an example of an audience analysis for one possible audience group - front line employees.

Start with what you know. These front-line employees have limited access to email, and the best way to communicate with them is via team huddles or meetings with their managers. They also have regular access to a break room area with a communication bulletin board. Now that you know what communication channels are available, what is the best way to communicate with them?

Based on this audience, I would first determine how and if it is possible to get information to front line employees through a different method – maybe the team huddle. You need to be judicious with this channel because you probably aren't the only group wanting to get information into it. One approach could be to ask if you could include some info during a focus month. For example, let's say your ERG is the Black Professionals Group. One approach might be to ask if you could provide information to be included twice per week during Black History Month. Another option is to partner with other ERGs and request an ERG section in the huddle script.

Communication Plan

The next tool in your toolkit is the **ERG Communication Plan Template**.

> When putting together a communication plan, start with the event or launch date, and work backward.

Working backward from your event date or initiative launch date will allow you and the communications team to hone-in on when you want your communications to begin and ensure you have enough time to get the messages out. For an event, I would suggest you start communicating no later than 30 days out. If it is a large event, an initiative, or program launch, you should begin communicating no later than sixty to ninety days out.

> *Be creative with messaging. Use teasers, visuals, newsletters, company intranet sites, team huddles, email, text, and other channels to help get the message out.*

Templates, Template, Templates

The best way to ensure communications happen regularly and fall within your company's brand standards is to have approved templates. In addition to the tools discussed above, the **ERG Handbook Companion Workbook** also includes the following templates: **ERG Communication Toolkit**, **ERG New Member Welcome Email**, **ERG Newsletter**, and **Social Media Plan**. Templates are an easy way to help volunteer communicators feel more confident doing their job and executing impactful communications.

Another tool that is important for any communication toolkit is Writing Tips. The **ERG Communication Writing Tips** in the **ERG Handbook Companion Workbook** can be used by those with a communication background as a refresher. For those without a communication background, it serves as a guide.

The earlier you start communicating, and the more channels you use will give you the best chance to get people to your events and the best chance of success.

If you are saying to yourself, "This is too much work, or, good grief Aimee did you forget the communications team is all volunteers?" No, I didn't forget, and I promise if you start with the end in mind and use the tools provided in the **ERG Handbook Companion Workbook**, your ERG will be communicating like a professional in no time.

Chapter 16 – What's Programming Got to Do with It?

Well, the short answer is...EVERYTHING! You can have all your leadership in place and be ready to set sail, but if you don't get participation from your members, what is the point? Without well-thought-out programming, your ERG will never have a real **impact** and create a **real** inclusive workplace.

If you are running an Affinity Group (AG), much of your programming might center around social activities. If you are running an ERG, your programming can still have a social component, but it needs to be more structured and tied to the ERG's mission and vision, which should link directly to the company's pillars, values, vision, and brand.

The best way to develop a program plan for a new group is to survey the members. Ask people what they are interested in, what they would attend, volunteer for, and, most importantly, what they think would help move the work environment towards being more inclusive.

Who else at your company has information that might be useful in building programming for your ERG? For instance, Learning and Leadership Development teams may have insights on what time of day people are most likely to sign up for (and actually attend) workshops. ERG leaders can share best practices on the location and timing of their most successful programs.

Programming and Events

Programs and events are internally or externally focused.

Examples of internal programming/events - luncheons, brown bag lunches, virtual meetings, social meetings, joint events with other ERGs, happy hours, tabling events, and celebrations of diversity weeks or months.

Examples of external programming/events - Habitat for Humanity build, coat drive, food drive, marching in a parade, and working a booth at a festival.

To ensure programming is successful, leadership at the national level needs to provide guidance and tools to local teams and empower them to schedule their own community events. However, the guidance needs to include structured oversight to ensure that local members feel empowered, operate within professional parameters, and represent the brand and the company well. The **Event in a Box Template** is an easy way to offer that guidance while still empowering members/teams.

Programming should be an opportunity to be creative and innovative without disregarding *tried and true* programs or events. The right balance between the two is important in creating and maintaining solid programming and ensuring there is enough variety available for every member to want to be engaged.

Community Events

As an ERG, you need to connect with your community – to determine in which events, festivals, parades, conferences, social settings, volunteer opportunities should you engage? This type of connection also needs to be made at the chapter levels. Empowering chapters to go out into communities they serve is a great way to start. Some good examples of community involvement:

- LGBTQ+ ERG partnering with AIDS Lifecycle to create a team to ride and raise money
- Women in Tech ERG partnering with Girl Scouts to create a technology badge
- Black Professionals' Group partnering with a local high school to offer resume writing tips and mock job interviews

A good partnership source is your ERG members. Many of your members are probably connected with a great organization resulting in a successful partnership for them and the ERG.

Tabling Events

The tabling event is a valuable tool in recruiting members and getting information about your ERG out to people who might not know it exists. It can be as simple as setting up a table in your building's high traffic area and staffing it during lunch. Getting out and talking to potential members is essential because you are just preaching to the choir with current members within an ERG. Having an organized opportunity to talk up the ERG can be important for current members' engagement and beginning connections with potential new members.

Diversity Months and Days

Another programming opportunity is celebrations of diversity-focused months or specific days focused on diversity topics. These diversity-focused events are also opportunities for ERGs to partner together. For example, Pride month is a great time for LGBTQ+ ERGs to partner with Black Professionals' ERGs to offer a program on the contributions Black LGBTQ people have made as members of both communities. To get started, check out the **Diversity Months and Days List** in the **ERG Handbook Companion Workbook**, but feel free to do your own research to find others that might fit with your ERG. Remember to be creative and innovative.

Having Courageous Conversations

ERGs are in a unique position to help lead the way in bringing issues to the forefront, especially issues that people might not be comfortable talking about. There are several ways to foster courageous conversations. ERGs can create bridges between leadership and employees and between ERGs to create a brave space to have conversations that will create steppingstones toward real change. I was surprised during a discussion on racism to hear how black colleagues were as uncomfortable as their white colleagues but for different reasons. Hearing their reasons gave me a whole new perspective. These kinds of a-ha moments are where real change begins.

> *Uncomfortable conversations are difficult for everyone. The key is to have a well thought out plan to ensure everyone feels heard, and conversations are productive -- not just 'bitch' sessions.*

Bringing in an external skilled facilitator might be your best bet to ensure successful and powerful, Courageous Conversations.

The Power of Storytelling

The fastest way to connect with your members and potential members' hearts and minds is through authentic storytelling. The most authentic and compelling storytelling comes from people who are willing to be vulnerable and share a story about themselves. An example of an event where you can use storytelling is a training and panel session. This session usually starts with a moderator sharing information on a topic and then having three or four panelists share their stories about how this topic impacted their lives. Two examples:

- Provide information on the history of systemic racism and then have panelists share how systemic racism impacts their lives.
- Provide information on LGBTQ+ history and terminology and then follow that with three panelists representing different sexual orientations and gender identities, sharing their stories.

Real-life Example: Equinix WeConnect

Equinix Employee Connection Networks (EECNs) created an amazing event called WeConnect. The purpose of WeConnect was to educate and inform people about the challenges of systemic racism. This 24-hour long event covered six time zones using an open Zoom line with videos, open chat, and breakout rooms. The event was employee-led, and the session categories included Courageous Conversations, Awareness, Wellbeing, and Celebration & Fun. Each of Equinix's six EECNs led at least one Courageous Conversation.

These quotes from participants sum up the power of the event:

"It is so good to work for a company that really believes in Diversity, Inclusion, and Belonging... gives me reassurance and the confidence to talk about things I would never have raised at work."

"Yesterday was one of the best days of my Equinix career, and I have been here for almost six years. The vulnerability, emotions, stories, authenticity, sharing – I canceled my day and stayed on (and what a finale!)."

This event demonstrates the power of storytelling and how ERGs can empower others to change what they want to see in the workplace and the world.

Programming Just for Members

ERGs are about creating an inclusive environment for everyone, including allies. However, there are times when programming needs to focus only on ERG-specific diversity. I recently heard an interesting way to do this – *Brave Space* and *Safe Space* programming. Brave Space programming is for all the ERG members, including allies, while Safe Space programming is only for the community members represented by the ERG. This model allows the ERG to serve the community they represent by giving that community a Safe Space to talk or work together. Having Brave Space activities ensures that allies understand what is needed to be more supportive and productive. Making ERGs inclusive is essential, but not at the expense of those represented by the ERG.

Vetting Speakers and Panelist

Making sure you vet your speakers or panelists is critical. If you are bringing in an external speaker, you should ask for a few references and a recent speech or presentation video. Make sure references and videos are no more than a few years old: the more recent, the better. A good place to look for speakers is a local speakers' group like Toastmasters, the National Speakers' Association (NSA), and Boston's Best Speakers

> Find out if your company has a process for vetting speakers and vendors and get familiar with it ASAP. When hiring someone to speak to or work with your ERG, you want to follow company policies and procedures for writing contracts, making payments, and more.

A good rule of thumb when hiring external speakers is 'you get what you pay for.' That is not to say that someone offering to speak for free will be bad. If someone is speaking for free, you should use the same vetting process outlined below.

In addition to references and videos, you might want to:

- Ask for a copy of their presentation at least a week in advance of the event date.
- Schedule a meeting with the presenter/speaker to go over their presentation slides and ask any questions. If you have members within the ERG who know the topic, include them in the meeting.
- Be sure the presenter is familiar with the technology they will be using. Nothing is more frustrating than having a presenter who is fumbling around with their presentation.
- If it will be a virtual session, do a dry run and make sure your presenter knows how to present in this format. It is not just about the tech, but also how to engage with the audience.
- Ask how the audience will be able to engage with the presenter. Should questions be submitted ahead of time? Will they be able to ask a question directly? Will they use the chat feature?
- Check out groups like the Employee Resource Group Leadership Alliance (www.ERGleadership.com), who have vetting tips and a list of vetted speakers and topics focused on ERGs and diversity.

For internal speakers or panelists, be prepared to do a bit more handholding, especially if they are publicly sharing a personal story. I recommend:

- Giving a time limit for speaking (3 to 5 minutes),
- Giving an outline of key points, you would like for them to address

- Offering to review their talking points with them before the event

This behind-the-scenes work will help ensure presenters/panelists are well prepared, and the end product will be a cohesive and engaging event.

Chapter 17 – To Measure or Not to Measure

Metrics is a word that makes ERG leaders run screaming from the room - (or at the very least elicits an audible groan). The thought of creating metrics for an ERG can be daunting, but it doesn't have to be. You can start small, and then as your ERG evolves, you can change what you measure. Here is the thing about metrics: If you don't measure, how do you know what's working and what's not? If you don't measure it, how do you show the value the ERG brings to its' members, the company, and the community you serve? What's measured gets attention and funding.

> *You don't have to measure everything but start by measuring something.*

Start with easy points to measure:

- How many members does your ERG have?
- What is the geographic makeup of membership? Break this down by location and further break it down by line of business or department.
- How has membership increased over time?
- How many events did the ERG sponsor this year? How does that compare with past years?
- What was the attendance/participation in any ERG sponsored events? How does that compare year over year?

Communication is also something you can measure. To help with this, check out the **ERG Communication Dashboard Template** in the **ERG Handbook Companion Workbook**.

Outline what communication goals you set for the year and then outline what you did. You should add what goals you have set for the next year on the dashboard's year-end version.

Charts are always an easy way to show what you have done and how it compares to previous years. You can measure:

- Number of articles the ERG posted to your company's intranet site

- Number of spotlights or features the company did on the ERG
- Number of email communications or messages sent to the membership
- The open rate of emails sent
- Number of page views of your ERG's intranet page

Return on Investment (ROI)

Most ERGs, especially well-established ones, want to measure the return on investment for the company. ROI can be more challenging to quantify, but not impossible. You just have to dig a little. Human Resources information can help measure ROI, but there can be a great deal of concern and caution about what information HR is willing to share. This caution is understandable because much of the information is confidential. (There is hope.) Asking for data as an aggregate or insights rather than raw data may work for you.

> *When asking HR/Legal for shared data, be very clear about why you're asking, what you will use it for, and who will have access.*

When you can make a strong business case for the need for data, you're more likely to obtain it. For instance, if an Asian-focused ERG is creating a leadership development program, it's useful to understand the spread of Asian teammates across company levels, roles, and businesses as part of the scoping phase to ensure your program planning is on track and scalable. You don't need individual line items or details – you need the themes and highlights.

Real-life Example: Melinda makes her case with data

When it came to gender diversity, Melinda had become frustrated with the leaders at her company. They spent a lot of time talking about their progress, but Melinda didn't see it materialize in promotions. Melinda wanted to figure out a way to get the data to show the real picture of where the company was when it came to gender diversity.

She knew there would be pushback if she made an official request to get HR data, so she decided to be scrappy. She asked members of the Women's ERG team to count and report the number of men and women in different roles across the company. Next, Melinda made a single slide that showed the ratios of women to men at each level. The numbers looked okay at the lower levels, with 1 or 1.5 men for every one woman. The data showed a massive discrepancy at the more senior levels - up to 13 men for every one woman. The data also showed there were no women at one level.

Melinda took that slide and presented it to the company's leadership team, and they were stunned. The numbers were bad, but what was worse – the story they told was so counter to who leadership was and how they wanted to be viewed as a brand and employer. The *scrappy slide* got a roadshow of its own across every office and became a huge catalyst for the conversation to drive real change and the role every man and woman, at every level, had in making that happen.

This story illustrates how you can gather data on your own and present it to create a real impact.

Let's look at the pillars/areas of focus from **Chapter 7** and see how you can measure your impact against these. The below pillars are a guide; if your pillars/areas of focus are different, find the metrics that align to your ERG specific pillars. The difference in pillars is not important; choosing what to measure and measuring it are key.

Workplace Environment / Culture

- Number of members attending the events/total membership?
- Create a SHORT survey for participants to complete. Two of the questions should be: 1) Rate the effectiveness of the event, and 2) How likely are you to do something differently because of attending this event?
- Increase in event participation year over year

Community

- Number of community events your ERGs participate in
- Number of participants over total membership
- Visibility in the community – For example, Hispanic ERG sponsors a booth at a Hispanic event. There were 6000 participants so that the ERG could reach 6000 people with the company brand.
- Number of interactions over the number of total participants = interaction percentage

Recruiting

- Number of members participating in recruiting events over total membership
- Number of participants ERG members interacted with over the total number of participants

- Number of recruits who accepted a job over total number recruited

Professional Development

- Number of professional development programs/events held
- Members attending professional development events over total membership
- Career Advancement: ERGs should identify members who have advanced their careers due in part to their participation in an ERG program or initiative. Write up at least three of these success stories and submit them to the D&I or HR department and to the company intranet site for possible publication.

Business Strategy

If you don't have goals aligned to the company's business strategy, this pillar can be tricky – but that doesn't mean you should not look for ways to measure the impact the ERG is having on the business. If you do have goals aligned to the business, then determine what you measure using those goals as a starting point.

Additional Metrics to Consider

- Member Engagement: ERG active members over ERG total members x 100
- Employee Turnover Rate (ETR): This is easier to measure if HR is willing to supply info to the ERG(s) or calculate this metric for ERGs. However, you can do a pretty good SWAG of this by keeping up with members who leave the company over the average total number of employees.

Employee Satisfaction

Many companies conduct regular employee satisfaction or engagement surveys. Requesting to include a question in the survey to determine the number of ERG members would be a great place to start. Next, having a question focusing on the impact ERGs have on overall employee engagement can help demonstrate ERGs ROI for the company. Another option is to create a survey for your ERGs members to gauge their level of satisfaction with the ERG(s) and find out how much ERG opportunities help increase employee engagement.

Regardless of what you choose to measure, those measurements should be precise, meaningful, and aligned to the ERG's mission and goals. Metrics are also a great way for multiple ERGs to collaborate to assess the overall impact ERGs have on employee engagement. Again, aligning some measurements to the pillars your company wants you to support will go a long way in demonstrating the ERG's value to members, executives, and executive sponsors. It can also show the value to your company's brand, which, in turn, impacts shareholders, customers, clients, and employees.

Chapter 18 – Creating Reports

When thinking about creating reports, many people go back to their paid job ideas of what reporting is and how it should look. This is not necessarily bad, but how your organization reports out versus how you report out as an ERG should be very different. The good news is that reporting out for your ERG can be easy and offers the opportunity to be creative.

As I talked about in **Chapter 17**, it is important to decide what you will measure and how you will measure it. The next question is how you present what you have measured. What would make this easier? Reporting templates, of course!

Here are some things you should consider creating reports for:

- Timeline of goals and where you are with those goals
- Key accomplishments
- Gaps or areas of opportunity
- Areas of focus/pillars aligned with goals
- Ongoing alignment with areas of focus/pillars
- ERG/chapter self-assessments

These are certainly not everything you might want to report on, but the list above is a great starting point.

Start with the end in mind. Knowing what you are measuring will help determine how and what you report out.

Why All This Reporting?

Reporting is your opportunity to showcase what the ERG is doing well and where things could use some improvement. Showcasing what you are doing well can help in making funding requests and recognizing the ERG's work and its members. Acknowledging an initiative or pillar that needs some extra focus demonstrates transparency. Remember, if you don't acknowledge an issue or problem, then chances are it won't get addressed or fixed.

ERG Goals and Focus Template

This template demonstrates how the ERG mission, focus areas, and goals are all aligned. It should be created at the beginning of the year and updated quarterly. For the end of year reporting, it is beneficial to outline your progress in completing each of the goals set for that year. If there are incomplete goals, it is important to call that out and give a reason.

Examples:

Goal: Create and launch a mentoring program (This is a two-year goal; the current completion rate is 50%.)

Goal: Increase membership by 10% (Membership increased by 7%, and we are looking at lessons learned to better understand why we could not reach this goal.)

Being transparent when talking about achieving your goals is important because it creates credibility for the ERG and its leaders.

ERG Report Out Summary Template

This template can be used at both the national and chapter levels and calls out key accomplishments, focus areas, and gaps. I recommend updating this quarterly.

I understand the tendency for ERGs not to bring up gaps and focus solely on accomplishments, but please don't try and sweep gaps and issues under the rug. Your executive sponsors are there to help you, and they can't help if they don't know the issues and gaps.

Pillar Alignment Heat Map Template

Heatmaps are a quick and easy way to show where you are and what areas need attention. Like the **ERG Report Out Summary Template**, this template is for the national ERG and ERG chapters. I recommend updating quarterly or at least twice a year. If you find you are green in every column, you need to take a hard look at why that is the case. Have you ever been a member of a team that meets all deadlines and goals? Let's face it; no ERG is great at everything. It is okay to be red and yellow in some areas if you understand why and have a plan to move toward green.

ERG Quarterly Executive Summary Template

This report is a snapshot executive summary that executive sponsors can use to promote the ERG. The ERG leadership team can also use this to send to the D&I Office and other executives that support the ERG. This template is a snapshot of where the ERG is and aligns the mission, accomplishments, pillars, and work to support the pillars. The membership data is a snapshot of the number and location of members.

You might be thinking, "Aimee, this executive summary only lists three pillars, and we support five or six." Great observation. The reason is that as an ERG leader and leadership team, you can't focus on everything if you want to accomplish anything. It is important to pick two or three priorities or pillars you will focus on and align your initiatives and programming under those. Having two or three priorities doesn't mean you can't have work aligned to other priorities or pillars, but focusing on the two or three instead of five or six will enable you to create measurable impact. Measurable impact is what it is all about!

Now that we have discussed the reporting templates let's talk about the who, what, why, where, and how.

Who Is Going to Do All This Reporting?

ERG leaders can't do everything, so this is where your administrative/business support team comes in. The data gathering and reporting function should be the responsibility of this team. Your leadership team may eventually grow to have a reporting or data lead or committee.

What to Measure

The ERG leadership team, working with the executive sponsor, should decide on data to be gathered and how to use these or other reports.

Where Do We Get the Data? How Do We Get It?

For the templates discussed in this chapter, the data comes from information the ERG collects and tracks.

Chapter 17 is your resource for getting the data you use in creating the reports outlined in this chapter.

These reporting templates are not the end all be all of reporting but can provide a solid framework for your ERG to begin the routine of reporting and allow you to make the reporting your own.

Part IV.

Thrive

Chapter 19 – Thrive

Congratulations! Can you believe it? You have led your ERG into the next phase in the *Inclusive Space™ ERG Progression Model*, Thrive. I hope you didn't experience many growing pains to get to this point, but if you did, congratulations on managing through and bringing the ERG forward. Thrive is my favorite phase – but that doesn't mean growing pains go away. Some important points to remember:

- Just like in Grow, you can't make everyone happy, so don't try to.
- I hope you have learned from your mistakes and your leadership team learned from any of theirs. Continue to learn from them and document issues so that future leaders don't repeat those mistakes.
- Have you surrounded yourself with people who have skills that you don't have or who are good at things that you aren't? Did you refrain from micromanaging and let them use their skills to do their thing? If you have, then stay the course. If not, it is never too late to start. A solid

leadership style will be the key to taking your ERG into the Thrive Phase and beyond.

Your ERG is in the Thrive Phase; now what? During this phase, you will focus on:

- Ramping up your metrics
- Developing and implementing a multi-year plan
- Making talent planning routine
- Developing your process for launching ERG chapters
- Recruiting and engaging allies
- Keeping all the balls in the air with everything you implemented during the Grow Phase

Metrics

At this point, metrics and reporting should be a routine practice. The Thrive Phase is the time to up your metrics game. Now would be a great time to revisit **Chapter 17** and look for ways to take your ERG's metrics and reporting to the next level.

Develop and Implement a Multi-year Plan

Now that the ERG is beginning to Thrive, it is time to plan for the future using a Multi-Year Planning process. With the information and tools in **Chapter 20**, you and your leadership can brainstorm, prioritize, document, and align a multi-year plan and make it a regular routine. Creating and implementing a multi-year plan is your best defense against trying to boil the ocean. My friend and former co-lead, Crystal, and I have said we wished we would have developed and routinized multi-year planning sooner. The good news is you and your leadership team can, and by doing so, can have a greater impact than you ever imagined.

Creating a Talent Pipeline

Leadership burnout can be a real issue for ERG leaders. It is also essential to bring in new leadership to help the ERG continue to Thrive. Don't wait too long to begin a talent planning process. I trust your organization does talent planning, thereby creating talent pipelines. ERGs need to do this also. Instead of learning it the hard way, **Chapter 21** is full of information, tools, and templates to get you on your way to creating the talent pipeline your ERG deserves.

> *Small organizations can create a talent pipeline across ERGs. You will still realize the benefits but not overtax individual ERGs to make separate talent plans.*

Develop a Process for Launching ERG Chapters

Your ERG can create a more significant impact by empowering teammates to organize and launch chapters in the communities where they live and work. **Chapter 24** provides the tools and templates to extend the reach of your ERG's mission and vision by making chapter creation a repeatable process that will set new chapters up to be successful.

> *If small organizations don't need to create chapters, they can focus their efforts on increasing membership and educating current members.*

Recruiting and Engaging Allies

Serving as the first ally to co-lead a well-established LGBTQ+ ERG and co-developing and leading a wildly successful Ally Program, allyship is where my heart is. I have learned a great deal about recruiting, communicating, and educating allies from the ground up. **Chapter 23** is designed to help you set-up your ERG and its members to recruit allies. Hopefully, this chapter will help you make allyship a priority within your ERG development. The end goal is for ERGs to work together to expand the definition of allyship beyond just a single marginalized community.

Building on the Grow Phase

Bringing your ERG this far is a great accomplishment, but it is not the time to rest on your laurels or turn the focus solely on what should be happening in the Thrive Phase. How do you keep all the balls in the air and still move forward? You make sure you don't neglect the work already done in the Grow Phase. Don't forget to nurture the relationship with your executive sponsors. The tools in **Chapter 10** can become a routine that you use and revisit every six months or annually.

Schedule time to check in with your executive sponsors about what is working and what could be improved.

As the ERG begins to Thrive, communication becomes more critical than ever. Communication processes should be functioning well at this point, but there are still opportunities to review and improve. Remember, ERGs are a great place to stretch creative muscles and think outside the box. Apply these two actions to your communications.

Just like in the Grow Phase, there will be 'stormy' times in Thrive. As ERGs develop and implement the multi-year planning process, some leaders and members might not be satisfied with the ERG's direction. Don't discount different viewpoints about the direction of the ERG. Make sure different views are heard and considered but don't allow those viewpoints to slow down the forward momentum. Just like in Grow, you might lose members who decide the direction of the ERG doesn't align with their goals – again, that's okay. The ERG will thrive if the work, initiatives, and multi-year planning remain aligned to the ERG vision and goals.

> *The multi-year plan is an excellent opportunity to check in and see if your ERG's goals, initiatives, and objectives have changed and if your ERG continues to align to the mission and vision, and the pillars.*

Don't be afraid to correct your course. When something doesn't go as planned, strong leaders acknowledge the shortcoming and use lessons learned to change the plan or the direction. Sometimes things happen that you have no control over, so use what you do have control over to stabilize the plan and move forward.

And lastly, thriving ERGs are doing exciting and impactful work. Remember to pause to recognize and celebrate successful events, impactful work, and dedicated volunteers.

Chapter 20 – Pulling It All Together

After a couple of years of attending the Out & Equal conference, my ERG co-lead and I felt we were at a precipice. Attendees came back each year with tons of energy, ready to take on everything and conquer the world. After the conference high wore off, and it was time to face balancing their paid jobs with their non-paid passion jobs, things quickly slowed down, and some projects even ground to a halt. We all faced another issue during the conference high; we all agreed to take on a lot more than we could do.

My co-lead Crystal and I decided to sit down and figure out how to harness the longer-term buzz. We focused our energy on a few well thought out priorities and made a plan focused not only on the present-day but also on the future. We both knew that continuing to change priorities every year wasn't helping us move the needle or allowing us to create the impact we knew we could. From this experience, we learned the value of implementing a multi-year planning process.

The four stages of Inclusive Space's multi-year planning process are:

- Brainstorming ideas
- Prioritizing those ideas
- Laying out the plan
- Aligning the plan to the pillars and across teams

Brainstorming

Brainstorming is an excellent exercise for several reasons. The most important is engagement, innovation, and being heard (plus for our leadership and us, it was just lots of fun). Brainstorming can also get out of control quickly. The **ERG Multi-Year Planning Brainstorming Worksheet** will help you keep things under control. Next, prioritize the output of brainstorming using the **ERG Multi-Year Plan Prioritization Worksheet** and the **Four Quadrants Template**. I will cover these two steps in the **Prioritizing Your Plan** section.

The Multi-Year Planning questions to consider for brainstorming:

- If there were no barriers, what are the top ten initiatives you would want your ERG to change or implement? If money, time, and resources were not an issue, then what could you do? This is what I refer to as blue-sky thinking.
- Which of your ten initiatives will take considerable time and effort? (Big Rock items) Even though you are just brainstorming, Big Rock items are something you need to give serious consideration. Having a high-level understanding of what it would take will make prioritizing much more manageable.
- Which of your ten initiatives could be accomplished quickly or with minimal effort? I call this low hanging fruit. What is something out there almost ready to be picked but needs some minor tweaks or a small influx of resources to bring it to fruition? With these types of projects or initiatives, people can feel a sense of accomplishment. In turn, it can help keep them engaged longer and allow time and energy to work on more intense alternatives.
- From your list, what would you consider to be cultural change? – Cultural change initiatives are important to identify since the Workplace pillar is one where your ERG should spend significant resources and time. These items will most likely be the ones requiring most of your resources (money, time, and people) and will take the longest to complete. After all, changing culture doesn't happen overnight.

- What barriers to implementation do you think exist? (These could vary from initiative to initiative.) You do not want to go through the entire multi-year planning process, then get to the end of the process and have an "oops" moment. Implementation barriers are real. You overcome some obstacles; however, some you can't overcome right now because the timing is not right. You need to think through and be realistic about these types of issues.

Prioritizing Your Plan

Now that you have finished brainstorming, you are ready to start prioritizing your brainstorming outputs. Prioritization is a two-step process.

- First step: You can use the **ERG Multi-Year Plan Prioritization Worksheet**. This exercise will help you and your leadership hone in on what you can do and what you can't do.
- Second step: Take the outputs of the **ERG Multi-Year Plan Prioritization Worksheet** and use the **Quadrant Worksheet** to begin to prioritize by placing these outputs in one of four quadrants. Quadrant I is for those ideas that are Important/Urgent; in Quadrant II should be ideas that are Important/Not Urgent; Quadrant III is ideas that are Unimportant/Urgent, and finally, Quadrant IV is for items that are Unimportant/Not Urgent.

ERG prioritization questions to ask:

- What kind of tasks/initiatives do your ERG leaders and members spend their ERG-focused time on currently? – Be honest about where leaders and members spend their time, especially if they spend time and resources focused on initiatives and projects not aligned to the ERGs mission and vision. Do you feel your ERG is making measurable and meaningful progress on the prioritized initiatives (aggregated from the top ten list)? Again, this is the time for honest conversation, discussion, and debate.
- What kinds of tasks/initiatives are your ERG leaders and members spending ERG-focused time on that do not align with your prioritized initiatives? Understanding this is critical to ensure that you are using your resources to create the greatest impact.
- Why are you/they spending time this way? It could be that some members have decided to do their own thing. It could also be because of a lack of guidance and clear expectations.
- How can you work together to accomplish what you agree are the most impactful (Big Rock) initiatives?
- What does this mean for other top ten initiatives (personal list or collective ERG list)?
- If you solicit more assistance/resources, how would you align ERG members' time? This is a high-level discussion but will feed the project planning process.
- What are some barriers to aligning most of your resources to a limited number of the most impactful (Big Rock)

initiatives? If you are aware of the obstacles, you can avoid them or plan to overcome them.

- What are some benefits to focusing on a greater number of smaller/easier/quicker initiatives vs. fewer Big Rock initiatives? Possible reasons: smaller quick initiatives show immediate results, which can increase engagement and demonstrate value.

- How might you overcome objections to not focusing on what other ERG members want? Your leadership team must have this discussion before rolling out the plan so that leadership presents a united front when engaging others in the plan. If there are questions about whether to include an initiative, answers should be the same regardless of who answers them.

- What are some strategies for maintaining discipline around the multi-year plan your ERG deploys? Strategies could include quarterly checkpoints, project checkpoints, etc. Whatever strategies you decide on need to be doable and repeatable.

- Prioritize your top ten on the four quadrants – I Urgent/Important; II Not Urgent/Important; III Urgent/Not Important; IV Not Urgent/Not Important. This exercise can take some time and shouldn't be rushed. Use this time to debate and discuss to ensurethe team comes to a consensus.

Laying Out Your Multi-Year Plan

Member engagement and executive support are critical to the success of the multi-year plan. To make this easier, use the **Documenting Your Multi-Year Plan Template**.

Your plan should be concise and straightforward. This template can be used as a walking around deck to introduce and market your plan.

To keep your plan focused and easy to understand, lay it out by:

- Primary Initiatives that are owned and controlled by the ERG
- Secondary initiatives owned and controlled by the ERG
- Key initiatives not owned by ERG but where the ERG has influence

For each of these categories include:

- Initiative Name
- Scope
- What you plan to achieve in the 1st, 2nd, and 3rd years
- For those initiatives where the ERG only influences, it is important to think through how you will influence in years one, two, and three.

Aligning

You have made it this far, congratulations! The last piece of the multi-year plan puzzle aligns ERG work to the pillars the ERG supports, and other groups or business lines focused on the same diversity characteristics. For this part of the process, use the ***Aligning Your ERG Multi-Year Plan to Pillars and Across Teams Worksheet***.

This final piece of the puzzle is important for two reasons: 1) you need to demonstrate how the ERG's work supports the required pillars or areas of focus, and 2) by aligning to other groups focused on similar work, you demonstrate an approach that is both tactical and strategic. This approach will go a long way in engagement with executive sponsors, the D&I office, and C-Suite executives supporting ERGs and D&I.

> *Aligning your plan to your pillars and across teams demonstrates that you are making good use of the organizations' resources and can serve as a proof point when requesting funding.*

The Process

Multi-year planning is not a one-and-done activity. The templates you have completed are living, breathing documents and should be reviewed and revised when necessary or at least twice per year. Things happen, and maybe you aren't making the progress you had hoped during year one, or perhaps you knocked it out of the park. Adjusting your plan keeps things on track and keeps you and your leadership team from over-promising and under-delivering (one of my pet peeves). Things don't always happen the way we plan, and course-correcting demonstrates well-developed leadership skills. It also helps to keep members and executive sponsors engaged and the work moving forward.

Chapter 21 – Talent Planning

"With great passion comes great burnout..."
— *Aimee Broadhurst*

Yes, I quoted myself. Why? Because I have seen and experienced burnout and want to help you and your ERG avoid it. A burned-out leader becomes disengaged from the work which they have previously been so passionate. One way to help prevent burnout is talent planning. Companies know the importance of talent planning – many times, roles and whole HR departments are focused on it. Why shouldn't an ERG have a similar focus?

Talent Planning for ERGs

To begin the talent planning process, start with the **ERG Leader Development Assessment – Talent Planning Template.** I suggest using this template to assess your national level ERG leadership first, and if you have ERG chapters, complete a template for all your chapter leaders. As the talent planning process becomes more ingrained, a chapter leader can facilitate it with their chapter leadership teams. Talent planning is how you begin building a leadership pipeline. To help you complete the ERG *Leader Development Assessment-Talent Planning Template,* I have included an example on the template.

Now you have the capabilities requirements, and you have identified the strengths, opportunities, and opportunity actions. The next step will be to determine who represents top talent in ERG leadership.

By consolidating information from the completed *ERG Talent Planning - Leaders Development Assessment*

Template, national leaders, and executive sponsors can easily determine top talent.

The next step is to complete the **ERG Top Talent Quarterly Review Template**. Use the competencies from your ERG leadership model to fill in the competencies on the template's right-side. Next, beginning on the left side, add each person's information. Finally, you need to determine where everyone is performing for each competency (either red, yellow, or green). Leaders can use the information gathered from the *ERG Talent Planning - Leaders Development Assessment Template* to determine where someone is functioning within a given competency.

The *ERG Top Talent Quarterly Review Template* offers an easy and visible way to see who your top talent is. The template also shows their areas of expertise and areas of opportunities, and it offers a quick visual of how your top talent stacks up. Use the final piece of this process only for top talent.

Now that you know where your key talent is, you need to assess your gaps and fill those gaps. To assist in this next step is the **Talent Planning Assessment Worksheet**. This worksheet will help you answer important questions like:

- What are the most critical roles in your ERG?
- What core competencies stand out?
- What core competencies are weak, and where are you lacking?
- Who can help identify and recruit new talent?
- Do you think you can upskill your current key talent to fill those competency gaps?

As a reminder, confidentiality in the process is key. Therefore, this exercise should be between the ERG co-leads and their executive sponsors. After completing each of the worksheets and templates for talent planning, you have all the information you need to fill leadership and talent gaps in your talent pipeline and create a succession plan.

Make It a Process

The only way talent planning works is if it becomes a regular process. It cannot be a one-and-done activity. The goal is to build an ERG leadership talent pipeline that ensures continued success and allows leaders to serve their terms and roll off, knowing someone who shares their passion will step in and continue the work. It is encouraging that the current leaders and future leaders know all their hard work will not be lost because there are

198

no leaders to step in and continue to move the ERG forward.

Remember, those going through an ERG talent planning process already go through a much more rigorous talent and development process with their paid job managers. Many people might not understand why ERG talent planning is important for a non-paid job. They could also be concerned about how the information will be shared or used.

It is critical to set-up a transparent process and a clear set of guidelines before beginning. Some suggestions for setting up the process and guidelines:

Be Clear about the Intent

The intent is to help ensure a strong pipeline of leaders at the ERG national and chapter level. As long as you are clear about the how and the why of talent planning, getting people engaged and comfortable will be much easier.

Timing

In the beginning, I recommend doing talent planning quarterly, but as the ERG becomes established, it can be moved to a minimum of every six months. Quarterly is best because the length of terms for ERG roles is short, and circumstances change, causing volunteers to cut back the amount of time they can volunteer or some need to step away completely.

Smaller organizations may have longer terms for leaders, and talent planning will happen less frequently. For example, if your leaders' terms are three to five years, you might start with every six months and then move to an annual review.

Confidentiality Is Critical

ERG talent planning info should not be shared outside of the ERG, and those having access to the information should also be limited. The person or team put in charge of this process MUST operate at a high level of integrity. If confidentiality is compromised, the process is compromised; it will be difficult to recover the trust needed to make talent planning successful.

Taking Talent Planning to the Next Level

Talent planning and creating a talent pipeline for one ERG is great, but what if you could make not just a singular ERG specific pipeline but a comprehensive ERG leadership pipeline. This is possible if you roll out the process and tools across all the company's ERGs, and each ERG commits to the same standards and timing. Cross-ERG talent planning makes it possible to consolidate top talent info across all ERGs and then form a committee with an executive sponsor from each ERG. This committee would go through a similar process of reviewing the information and discussing top talent. This type of talent discussion would help formulate ways to use talent across the entire ERG space rather than just focusing on a specific ERG.

> *Using talent across the entire ERG space can be especially beneficial to smaller organizations.*

> *ERGs provide a great source of opportunity to build leadership talent across the organization, not just for the ERG.*

The Tale of Talent Surplus vs. Talent Gap

Let's look at an example of how a cross-ERG leader pipeline could work. Company XYZ has eight established ERGs. Seven of their ERGs have been in existence for 6-10 years and have worked together to create an ERG talent pipeline. The Disability Network is the newest ERG and has been around for two years. This new ERG is experiencing a gap in several key leadership roles. By having a cross-ERG talent pipeline, executive sponsors and other leaders can pull from the ERG talent pipeline to fill positions within the Disabilities Network ERG or find talent to mentor and grow the Disability Network's current leaders to fill the gaps.

The good news is that talent planning is effective, whether done by one ERG or a collaboration of all the ERGs. The most important way to ensure success is to have a process, communicate the process, commit to the process, and then DO IT!

Chapter 22 – Leadership Selection Dos and Don'ts

There are two schools of thought on leadership selection for ERGs – election or appointment. Over the last several years, many ERGs have been moving to the appointment approach, especially to select national and regional leadership. I am glad to see them move away from the election model to select ERG leaders. You don't want this to be a popularity contest and create hurt feelings and animosity. The election model could cause you to lose those in your leadership pipeline, which is a loss for everyone.

I think appointing these leaders is the way to go, and there are two ways to do this. One way, which I know works, is for the current leaders to select their successors. Leaders of an ERG understand who the top talent is in their ERG and across other ERGs. The leaders know what it takes to succeed and ensure their successor will take the reins and move the ERG forward. The other way is for the executive sponsors to work with the D&I office and current leaders to determine a slate of candidates. If the D&I office wants to put forth a slate of candidates for interview and selection, they should include current leaders in the interview and selection process.

A Saga of Two Leadership Selections

Part 1

An ERG was in the process of replacing both of its national co-leaders. The outgoing co-leaders, Martha and Raquel, had served for over four years. They were well known and respected, not only within the ERG they led but across the company. The plan was to replace Raquel first, and then six months later, replace Martha.

> *Rolling rotation is ideal for replacing national and chapter leadership and critical team leaders.*

Martha and Raquel had someone in mind as Raquel's replacement and started having conversations with her. Angela had been involved in the ERG for many years in a variety of roles. Many people knew and respected her and the work she had done. Angela agreed to become a national co-lead. So, Martha and Raquel announced her as the new co-lead replacing Raquel. Since Angela was a known leader and her reputation preceded her, Raquel and Martha easily inspired trust in Angela as the new national co-lead. Raquel stayed on for three more months to ensure a seamless transition.

Involve outgoing leadership in the selection process. They can be your best advocates for new leaders, especially if they feel included in selecting that leader.

Part 2

During Raquel's three-month transition period, the process began to select Martha's replacement. This time, however, Martha, Raquel, and Angela were not allowed to be part of the process to choose Martha's replacement. The process had changed. Executive sponsors and the D&I

office would be selecting Martha's replacement. Don't get me wrong; changing who would make the final selection was not a bad idea. It took the pressure off Martha, Raquel, and Angela having to find Martha's replacement. And, quite frankly, that isn't something that outgoing leaders should have to do by themselves. Issues arose when Martha, Angela, and Raquel were left out of the process.

Leo was selected to be Martha's replacement, which caught all three women off-guard. No one in the ERG knew Leo, and he had not been involved in any ERG in any role, including leadership. He was also at an executive level in the company. Again, not necessarily a bad selection, but some perceived it as the tolling of the bell regarding volunteer leadership development opportunities in ERGs.

Leo was announced, not by the outgoing co-leads like Angela had been, but by a C-Suite executive. Changing who made the announcement was not necessarily a bad change; however, optics should be a consideration when making these types of changes.

As soon as Leo was announced as the new co-lead, Martha, Angela, and Raquel were inundated with questions about who Leo was and what involvement/experience he had in ERGs. They were all three put in an uncomfortable position because they didn't know Leo or why he was selected to lead this ERG. What they did know was that he lacked leadership or sponsorship experience with any ERGs. This decision and process felt to many people like how managers and leaders are selected for paid jobs. And quite frankly, that is not what volunteers want within an ERG where they are so passionate.

Leader Selection - Day Job vs. ERG Role

Employees know how manager selection works in Corporate America. Likewise, employees understand why they don't get a say in that process. But when the same process is used in selecting and installing leaders in their volunteer work, members may become dissatisfied and leave the ERG because it feels like a corporate takeover. They may question if there is a hidden agenda, which then shakes the trust of the members. If people cannot feel safe to bring their authentic selves to the ERG table, it may lead them to reevaluate their place and their value within the company.

Current leaders are facilitating the work, and they understand the intricacies of their roles better than anyone. They also have their finger on the pulse of the membership. Current leaders' thoughts and opinions can be invaluable in selecting who will fill their roles. They can also be the best advocates for new leadership. They already have the members' trust and can inspire confidence in the new leadership if they are engaged and involved.

Not including current leaders in the process discounts their passion, leadership, and experience. It is as simple as that. When new leaders are announced, the ERG members look to the current leaders to answer any questions they have and facilitate a smooth transition. If current leaders don't have input in the selection process, they cannot honestly or truthfully endorse the new leadership, and ensuring a smooth transition becomes more difficult.

> *Outgoing leaders should ask to be included in the selection process for their replacement.*

Some might say, "Well, that is not how it works in business." Many times, new leaders are selected behind closed doors, and everyone needs to get on board. My response is, "That might work in the business where you are paying people to do their job, but it doesn't work well when selecting volunteer leaders."

> *The selection process for non-paid ERG leaders cannot be the same for paid job leadership selection.*

As I will cover in **Chapter 25**, managing volunteers is very different from managing people whose salary and benefits you pay. This fact is important for executive sponsors to understand. New leaders need to inspire and help the ERG and its members to continue to evolve and connect to their passion.

This real-life saga of two leadership selections demonstrates how important the leadership selection process is for ERGs. Discounting your current leaders' experience can negatively affect them, those they lead, and the ERG's functionality and longevity. In the long run, it can also impact employee loyalty and retention.

Chapter 23 – What Do Allies Have to Do With It?

Allies have a lot to do with it. In fact, many of the advancements in civil rights over the last century would not have happened without allies. A historical example would be the women's suffrage movement. With the patriarchy as the ruling majority, the women's right to vote would never have occurred had it not been for how women such as Elizabeth Cady Stanton, Susan B. Anthony and Carrie Chapman Catt (to name a few) included the recruitment of men in support of the cause. Those men influenced other men because, well, they were men. More recently was the fight for marriage equality. Without allies of the community standing up and fighting with the LGBTQ+ community, marriage equality would not have happened. Therefore, engaging allies with your ERG is important. The first step in engaging allies is defining what an ally is and what the community needs from its allies.

What You Can't See Can Hurt Others

You're probably thinking...what? My initial reaction when I titled this section was the same. Am I talking about microbes or tiny jellyfish or a truck you don't see until it hits you? The answer is none of those things. I am talking about visible allies, backers, and champions to those who don't enjoy the same rights and privileges. Being an ally is important, but if the people you support can't see you, how will you benefit them? How can you help if you aren't visible and aren't speaking up?

The bottom line...you can't. When someone is LGBTQ+ and they don't see visible allies where they work, then bringing their whole selves to work isn't an option. If a woman in technology doesn't see any of her male colleagues or managers supporting and standing up for women, is she going to feel empowered? If an executive making hiring decisions doesn't work to create a diverse candidate slate for a job opening, will diverse candidates have a chance of being hired? No, no, and no!

Hear ye! Hear ye! Allies Are Important!

I think I can best illustrate how important they are with two stories about transitioning at work.

> *Real-life Example: Allison transitions without support at work*
>
> Allison is transgender, a lesbian, wife, and proud grandmother. She has a very fulfilling life, but, in the beginning, she never imagined that was possible. When Allison knew it was time for her to begin to live her authentic self, she worked for Company A, where she started her career as Alexander.
>
> Alexander was very honest about the transitioning process and did his best to do all the right things to make the transition easy for his team and leadership. Leaders and teammates acted like they were okay with everything, but things quickly took a turn for the worse. As her transition began, Allison was relegated to a bathroom two floors up from her workspace.

She endured looks and was referred to by hurtful language and called names.

People like Allison risk being ostracized, ridiculed, passed over for promotions, physically assaulted, or even killed for being who they are. They have few legal protections and virtually no avenues of recourse.

Real-life Example: Kara transitions with the support of allies

Kyle had worked for Company B for over fifteen years before finding the courage to live out his authentic self as Kara. Kyle talked with his manager, who brought in someone from Human Resources. The difference in this story is that Company B had an Ally Program. Kara could go online and see who the allies were in her department, division, and business line.

Allies were physically visible with stickers and tent cards in their offices. Company B also had transgender benefits in place that Kara was able to use. Kara was not relegated to a bathroom far away from her office space. She did not have to endure the under-the-breath, bigoted comments. If she were to experience any of this, she knew she was in an Inclusive Space™ with visible allies all around her.

Do LGBTQ+ ERGs Have the Market Cornered on Allyship?

Well yeah, they kind of do. Why is this true, and what can other ERGs learn from them? One big reason is sexual orientation and gender identity are not characteristics you can necessarily see. For example, when you and I meet (and I hope we do someday), you will immediately know some things about who I am. I am a woman but what you can't see or hear are that I am a wife with an amazing husband. I am a mom, daughter (the oldest), sister, stepdaughter, straight, cisgender, and I am known as the Galactic Ally (aka Champion) for the LGBTQ+ community.

Although you can't see my sexual orientation, you would know when you see the pictures on my desk. In a few minutes of conversation, you would know that I feel free to be who I am. In many cases, people in the LGBTQ+ community do not feel free and safe to be seen or heard. Many spend a lot of time, energy, and heartache, keeping their authentic selves hidden due to fear of exclusion and retribution.

Another reason LGBTQ+ organizations have done well with allyship is their ability to define what they need from their allies. I was leading a conversation recently about allyship, and by the end of the hour-long call, we discovered that most of the ERG leaders present realized their ERG had not defined what they needed from their allies. Wow! If you don't tell your allies what you need from them, it will be harder to attract them and get them involved in your ERG work.

So, what can other diversity groups learn about creating and welcoming allies and advocates? I remember a conversation with a D&I executive about creating an LGBTQ+ Ally Program at a Fortune 50 company. She was resistant, saying other ERGs need allies, too. I was hell-bent on creating this program and began to list all the reasons people of the LGBTQ+ community needed allies. In retrospect, I realize that she was right about other diversity groups needing allies.

Believe it or not, many people want to be allies but don't know how they are needed, and they don't know if they are welcome. One of the best ways to recruit allies is to make them feel welcome and let them know what you need from them. You will be amazed at how many people will reach out and become more engaged just because you let them know how they are needed and what they can do.

What Can Other ERGs Learn from the LGBTQ+ Community on Creating and Engaging Allies?

As an ally of the LGBTQ+ community, I understand the importance of being a visible ally. Still, I have also learned why it is important to be an ally to other marginalized communities.

Here is what I think other groups can learn from the LGBTQ+ community about engaging allies. First, people want to know that they belong and have a place. Making a case for ally recruiting should be at the top of your to-do list. It doesn't matter where your ERG or chapter is on the progression model. Educated and visible allies are one of the best voices any marginalized group can have. For example, being a straight ally for the LGBTQ+ community, my voice is more powerful with many because I have always had the right to get married. Also, I don't have to worry about being 'outed' at work.

We know that we tend to gravitate toward people we perceive to be just like us. If other people see me being an ally and see the impact that makes with LGBTQ+ coworkers, they are more likely to become an ally. Let's face it. Marriage equality didn't happen because only LGBTQ+ people were in decision making positions. Others joined in and supported their fight for equal rights and freedoms.

Now Is the Time to Become an Ally for All

As I am finishing this chapter, we are in the midst of a global pandemic, and we have all seen the horrible death of George Floyd at the hands of four Minnesota police officers. This horrific event is galvanizing allies in a way I haven't seen up to this point. The time for white allies to stand up for our black and brown brothers and sisters is long overdue. Being visible and speaking up now can be the difference between life and death.

Becoming an ally for the LGBTQ+ community was easy for me because I have LGBTQ+ family members. I want them to enjoy all the same rights and privileges I enjoy, and I know the difficulties they have suffered on a very personal level. But I cannot stand by and focus my allyship only on the LGBTQ+ community. We all must become an ally for EVERYONE who is suffering and marginalized in our society. As an ally, it is up to each of us to educate ourselves on the plight of others and then to make ourselves visible and speak up. When I say speak up, I mean SPEAK UP LOUDLY and TAKE ACTION! Nothing will ever change if allies do not become as enraged with injustice as those suffering the injustice.

Chapter 24 – Expanding an ERG through Local Chapters

As an ERG evolves and membership grows, the time will come when your leadership team will need to consider creating a structure to allow chapters to form.

Smaller organizations might not ever need to create chapters. This doesn't mean smaller organizations can't have thriving ERGs. Instead of developing chapters, focus your efforts on growing your membership, educating your current members, and recruiting allies.

If it is time for your ERG to begin the process of creating chapters, congratulations! The process must be simple, straightforward, and repeatable so that these new chapters can be successful right out of the gate.

Creating the Process

The best way to develop chapters is to start with the end in mind and work backward. Your end goal for a chapter is for it to be successful as soon as possible - that is where you need to start.

> When expanding ERGs with local chapters, design the process to be repeatable.

How does a successful chapter look? Successful chapters:

- Have active local membership
- Partner with local organizations
- Create and launch successful events and, most importantly, have a real impact in the community and location they serve

In my experience, beginning with a chapter application process will make it easier for both ERG leaders and those wanting to start a new chapter. An application process creates a level playing field, regardless of who or where the new chapter wants to begin.

Let's look at the type of information included in an application to create a chapter.

Applying to Start a Chapter

Some of these questions are similar to starting an ERG, which should not be a surprise. The new chapter process should ensure solid alignment between the ERG purpose and the chapter purpose. Also, chapters should be an extension of the ERG and not an opportunity to create a splinter group. I believe people start with the right intentions. Still, sometimes personalities and other factors will create an environment where people feel empowered to take the road less traveled and not in a positive way. With a well thought out application process, ERG leadership can create guardrails for new chapter startups and avoid micromanaging them in the future.

Using the **ERG Chapter Application Worksheet** in the **ERG Handbook Companion Workbook,** let's look at questions for the application process:

1. **What is the purpose of starting this chapter, and how will this chapter's creation benefit local employees?**

    A new chapter's purpose and benefits should align with the ERG's but can have a dash of a local or market-specific flavor. For example, the new chapter aims to serve ERG members locally by providing local programming and events. A benefit could be to offer more opportunities to get involved on a local level, better serve the communities supported by the company, and provide more ERG members leadership opportunities.

2. **How much interest does this location have (building, city, community) in starting a chapter of your ERG?**

    You need a minimum of 15 to 25 people to ensure a successful launch of a new chapter. You need people with passion committed to volunteering and serving, not just people who think it is a nice idea.

3. **Are there other ERG chapters in the location/market?**

    If there are other ERG chapters in the same location/area, new chapters should reach out to those chapters' leaders and schedule some time to talk with them. They are the first go-to resource. These leaders might also be willing to ask their members' thoughts on the chapter you're looking to start.

4. **Who and where are your potential members located? Do you have enough potential members who are in close enough proximity to attend local events?**

    The data most valuable here would likely need to come from Human Resources. Information to request would be the number of employees in the area or market; the number of employees currently members of ERGs or chapters; the number of employees currently members of your ERG.

5. **What support do you have from your organization's local or regional leadership to start this chapter? Do you have an executive sponsor in mind?**

Support from local and regional leadership is very important. Without that level of support, the chapter will never get off the ground. The executives supporting the start of the new chapter should be the first place to go to find the chapter's first executive sponsor.

6. **Who will make up the initial chapter leadership team?**

Just like when building a new ERG, a new chapter will need to create initial roles and corresponding job descriptions:

- Chapter co-leaders
- Business support leader
- Events leader
- Communications leader

These are the initial roles to be filled when establishing a new chapter, but more roles will need to be added as the chapter grows. The ***Roles & Responsibilities***

Worksheet in the ***ERG Handbook Companion Workbook*** can be modified and become a tool for developing your new chapter process.

7. **How will the chapter be launched?**

   The new chapter leadership needs to think through the best way to market to their local audience. Since membership is local, there might be an opportunity to have a launch event. This could be a social event or a volunteer event in the community.

8. **What are two or three goals the chapter has for the year?**

   Chapters need to focus on the launch, but it is also essential to look ahead to establish two or three goals to achieve in the first year. I suggest setting specific timing for achievement, as well. For example, launching the chapter is the goal for the first three months. Plan to accomplish the second goal in the first six months and the third by the end of the first year.

How about some good news now? There is no need to start from scratch. Chapters 8 and 9 are useful resources when you are creating a new chapter process.

Chapter Funding

ERG national leaders need to be able to discuss funding with the new chapter leaders. If your ERG is funded by D&I or HR, your new chapter leads need to know if they will get a piece of that pie and how that process works.

Real-life Example: Chapter budget guidelines help set expectations

At a Fortune 100 company, ERG chapters received an annual budget of $500 per chapter from the national ERG's budget. The national ERG Leadership team also set aside designated funds to distribute in support of initiatives.

Each chapter is required to submit an annual budget in January. This budget includes all funds the chapter leaders think they will need for all their events and programming and is usually over the $500 budget. This routine helps the ERG

National leadership team know each chapter's plans and financially what each chapter plans to spend.

For anything over the annual allotment, chapters must submit a request for additional funding.

Governance

A governance structure should include a monthly meeting between chapter leaders and national leaders. This meeting routine will ensure connectivity between national leaders and chapter leaders and allows new chapter leaders to get to know each other, allowing them to build meaningful relationships.

Chapter 25 – Leading Employee Groups: The Good, The Bad and The How

Have you ever been in a meeting where you are speaking English, but it feels like everyone hears you speak Spanish? Sometimes leading volunteers or being a volunteer can feel like this. What are the secrets to speaking the same language?

Leading Volunteers...Not Like Leading a Team

I have said this before, and I will say it again, leading volunteers is not like leading/managing people that are paid. Unfortunately, a lot of leaders don't grasp this concept. Those leading ERGs need to be different kinds of leaders and use a different set of leadership skills. You need to inspire people, tap into their passion for the mission, and MAKE THEM feel valued. You might be saying, "Well, I do that in my day job." Okay, maybe you do, but trust me, it is different when you're leading people who are not paid. Right or wrong, there is a particular loyalty that comes with a paycheck because the company is paying for someone's time and talents. There are expectations, performance plans, raises, and bonuses. People treat you differently and react to you differently if you have some say over their pay.

No need to run screaming, you can do this, and you can do it well. Keep reading!

Captain or Coach

On this ERG leadership journey, you might think of yourself as the captain of your ERG ship. Words are important, and sometimes people's image of a captain is someone barking orders at the members of a sailing team. That is not how you captain this ERG ship. So instead of being a captain, think of yourself as a coach. You might be thinking, "I really don't see a difference; coaches bark orders at their players." Maybe some do, but the best coaches know how to make their players feel valued as individuals AND as members of a team working toward a common goal. What you want and what a coach wants are the same thing: Everyone to feel valued and contribute to the team with their specific skill sets. As a coach, it is your job to help figure out those skill sets. If you followed my suggestions in **Chapter 12**, you have assembled a team of people and are very familiar with their skill sets. If not, this part is going to be more challenging for you. Before going any further, I suggest you meet with each team member and understand their skill sets.

Making the Game Plan as a New ERG Leader

I cannot emphasize the importance of understanding the way previous leaders did things before you. Understanding the ERG history is a crucial step in getting everyone on the same page. To start, make sure you have conversations with any leadership team members who are staying on to work with you. There need to be frank and honest conversations about what is working and what is not. Taking the time to have these conversations is not rocket science, but many leaders, even seasoned ones, don't do this. It can be the difference between a leader that inspires or one that people tolerate.

Real-life Example: Andre takes over as co-lead

A national co-lead for an ERG was moving on, and her replacement, Andre, was coming on board. Andre started with some strikes against him because no one knew who he was, and he had never been in a leadership role with an ERG. Andre came in and briefly met with outgoing leaders Cecilia and Samantha. This was a good start. Unfortunately, it quickly became apparent that Andre was out to prove why he was the right selection for this role. Andre's actions frustrated many members of the leadership team. What could Andre have done differently?

Having a meeting with the outgoing leaders was the right thing to do, but those meetings should have extended to individuals remaining on the team. At this stage, the right questions to ask are:

- What specifically do you do in your role?
- What do you like about your role?
- What do you dislike?
- If you could change one thing, what would that be?

In addition to asking these questions, Andre should have *listened more* and talked less. At this stage of the game, I cannot emphasize enough the importance of active listening. It's not always easy, but it is necessary. So, if you are not a good listener, know and acknowledge that going in. Make it a goal to work on becoming a better listener. **Chapter 26** has information on how to become an active listener.

Change, including new leadership, can be positive. If you try to make significant changes before you understand the work already underway, you will alienate the people you want to inspire.

Before you do anything, talk to your predecessor, and see how they did things. To get the current pulse of the ERG, talk with the current members and the leadership team.

> *Please don't come in with the attitude of trying to save the day!*

Boiling the Ocean...It Can't Be Done

This section's title is a phrase I have used thousands of times in my ERG leadership roles, and several times in this book. As a reminder, no matter how much passion and energy you have, you cannot do everything, and you cannot make everyone happy. You need to realize this going in so you don't waste time and energy.

To keep from boiling the ocean, you have to be realistic with yourself, your leadership team, and your members. After an event, like a conference, people are excited, invigorated, and ready to change the world. They are full of ideas and energy and volunteer for more than they can do, and more than the ERG has the resources to undertake successfully. I covered how to avoid this in **Chapter 20**. Now that you know the good, the bad, and the how, let's talk about the skills necessary not only to lead but to inspire.

Chapter 26 – When You Need to Take Charge

When You Need to Have Hard Conversations

There will be times when you need to have hard conversations with people within any leadership or managerial role. This is true when working with volunteers as well. Volunteers are often some of the most passionate and hard-working people with whom you will ever have the pleasure of working. They want to share their passion, knowledge, and insight into the causes in which they believe. Sometimes, passion overrides practicality, and a volunteer will bite off more than they can chew, leading to over-promising and under-delivering tasks.

Having managed volunteers in different organizations, I have learned other issues can skew some volunteers' motivation. For example, someone may not feel like they have control or power at home, work, etc. and decide to find a place to control, like in a volunteer role. As a leader, you can often do things to make this a win-win situation for everyone, but there are times when it just won't work out.

Real-life Example: Jonathan reinvents the wheel

Jonathan served as the communication lead for an ERG chapter in Florida. Communications were not a part of Jonathan's day job, so this role was an opportunity for him to build his communication skills. A communication toolkit and specific branding guidelines were developed and rolled out to educate and empower ERG communicators. Jonathan received the toolkit, guidelines, and mentoring from the chapter leadership but decided to do things outside of brand standards. I guess that Jonathan struggled with some other issues around power/control in his life, which caused him to channel that power/control into his volunteer role.

In many cases, this wouldn't have been a problem; however, it was in this case. The leaders of the Florida ERG chapter tried to handle the situation respectfully, such as referring him back to the toolkit, offering more training, support, and guidance. Jonathan continued not to comply and even filed a complaint with Human Resources.

Handling It

Okay, just because HR was involved, the ERG chapter leaders didn't panic, and if something like this happens to you, don't panic. The chapter leaders did everything right, including engaging their regional and national leadership. Together everyone decided to involve HR.

As a volunteer leader, do not be afraid to manage up and engage regional and national leadership. As an ERG chapter or national leader, you should feel comfortable engaging your executive sponsors when necessary.

> *Don't make managing up a regular occurrence. Trust your leadership skills, but don't be afraid to call in reinforcements.*

Remember, the ERG Represents Your Company

This section will be short and sweet. An ERG is an extension of your company and the employees of that company. As a leader of an ERG, remember to drive home this message with other leaders and members. This includes maintaining the company's brand in everything you do. Some companies' brand and marketing teams will give some leeway to ERGs developing collateral, communications, and logos, while some will not. As an ERG leader, it is your job to know what is allowed within brand compliance and communicate that to all leaders, including those responsible for member communications. Everyone needs to be diligent and accountable, without exception.

> *Find out if there are brand standards for ERGs and follow those standards. If they don't exist, help create them.*

If you need to create something different for your ERG, always consult branding. I recommend including someone from the brand team early in your discussions. It will save you time and lots of head and heartaches.

A Story

Back in 2011, I was attending my very first Out & Equal Workplace Summit in Dallas, Texas. At that time, I was leading communications for the LGBTQ+ Pride ERG. I met a young man named Daniel, who led the London LGBTQ+ Pride ERG at our company. There had been some murmurs throughout LGBTQ+ Pride that we needed to create an ally program. Daniel and I decided that we were going to be the ones to make that happen.

We knew it was essential to the program to create ways for people to be visible through the program. One way we decided to do that was with branded collateral. We wanted stickers for laptops and lapels, tent cards for desks, and a manual for being an ally—all this required branding. Luckily, one of my good friends was also my favorite brand policeman, Ric. Our goal was to work together and create a *win/win* for the program and the company's brand.

Branding and rules differed between the U.S. and the U.K., and branding differed between the major business lines. In the U.K., rules for the ERGs were not as strict as they were in the U.S. Although there were many meetings and some gnashing of teeth (actually more like A LOT of teeth-gnashing,) in the end, we were able to work together with the brand team to create something that we were all very proud of and proved to be very successful. The rest, as they say, is history!

Involve your brand team in discussions at the very beginning. You will be glad you did.

These are just two examples of the types of situations you might encounter as an ERG leader. The key to rising above these challenges is listening. Know when things are heading in the wrong direction and when you can handle it or when you need to call in reinforcements. One of the biggest lessons I learned is to let your passion fuel your work, but don't let it take over when you are making decisions.

Chapter 27 – Leading and Inspiring

In addition to being a former ERG leader, I am also a life coach. Being a life coach has helped me become a better leader, especially related to my ERG work. I hope I can impart some of the knowledge I have learned about being a coaching leader.

This chapter is for all ERG leaders whether you are a national, regional, or chapter level leader or leading a team (i.e., communications, engagement, social, administrative, etc.) If you develop these leadership skills, you will be well on your way to leading in your day job and your volunteer job.

Active Listening

Most people think they are good listeners; however, most people are not. To really listen, you need to quiet your mind and focus on what the other person is saying. Even as a trained coach and leader, I continuously work on my listening skills. Our 17-year-old daughter is the only person in our family who is naturally a good listener, and trust me; she came wired that way. I know she didn't learn it from her Dad, her sister, or me.

PRACTICE: While you are having a conversation, notice how many times you are focused on what you will say next versus actively listening to what the other person is saying.

I hope you discovered that you didn't focus on what you were going to say next because that means you are probably a good listener. When people talk to good listeners, they feel heard. Suppose you are already a good listener, congratulations. For those of us that aren't good at active listening, there is hope. Now that you are aware of where your focus is or isn't, you can challenge yourself and practice to change it.

Empowering

This one can be tough. The first rule of empowering is to surround yourself with people who are good at things you are not. Doing this makes empowering people so much easier. It also makes the job of leading easier and more fulfilling. Who doesn't want that?

This next story is mine, so I will not change the names to protect the innocent. Let me set the stage, my ERG co-lead, Crystal, and I were attending the Out & Equal Workplace Summit and had the opportunity to spend an entire day with some of our national, regional, and chapter level ERG leaders from across the world. During our time together, we broke up into task tables with the goal of each group coming up with a minimum of two ideas the ERG should move forward. This sounds great, right? Well, it was, and we all left on a conference-high and ready to take on the world.

Then came the problem. Everyone's conference-high wore off, and we were all back in our day jobs. Crystal and I knew we had to capitalize on the momentum created at the event. We also knew there was no way to implement all the initiatives, programs, and ideas that this incredible team of global ERG leaders had come up with to move forward. So, what did we do? We brought in Haley.

Haley knows Crystal and me very well – and she knows what we do and don't do well. Also, Crystal and I both know this about ourselves and each other. We knew we needed someone who would cut through our BS and keep us on task. We needed Haley. Haley is a project manager extraordinaire, cutter of the BS, and all-around spunky redhead. Haley is great at things that Crystal and I are not – and we both knew it. Haley was just one of the extraordinary teammates we brought on board and let them do what they do best.

This is an example of why surrounding yourself with people who are good at things you aren't. Letting others do what they do best is a mark of great leadership. In other words, learn to leverage your talent pool.

Picking Your Battles

The above phrase I have heard my entire life, especially during my career. It might sound simplistic, and it is. Simply put, you cannot take on everything and everyone that comes into your leadership path. If you try, you will burn out, and you will fail. It IS that simple.

Picking your battles can be as straightforward or as complicated as you want to make it. The best way I found to determine which battles to fight was to talk about it with my leadership partner and the ERG leadership team members. I also found it was essential to listen to the membership of the ERG.

Before you decide to go headlong into battle, ask members questions, and get some opinions on the impact something is having or may have on them.

With all this talk of battle, let's pause here. I don't want you to think as an ERG leader that you will continuously be picking and fighting battles. I mean, seriously, what fun is that? If I am honest, sometimes it was fun for me because my passion and activism fueled me. Yet, I understand that not everyone is the same, and not everyone deals with conflict in the same way.

Having a trusted confidante who knows you, your leadership style, and passion will keep you from picking the wrong battles or picking all the battles.

Real-life Example: An ERG leader picks her last battle

There once was a bathroom bill called HB2. With this bill's passage, transgender people were required to go to the bathroom aligned with their birth sex. A company in the impacted state came out with a middle of the road statement about this bill's passage.

The LGBTQ ERG leaders felt it wasn't enough, and they also heard this from their membership. The two ERG leaders got together to vent and decide if this was a battle they wanted to fight. After a lot of venting, commiserating, and sadness, the leaders made their decision. Although they both knew it could be risky to go up the chain and make this request, they knew it was the right thing to do. An email was prepared and reviewed, then reviewed, and then reviewed some more. One of the ERG leaders hit the send button. This story has a happy and sad ending.

The good news is the company sent out a revised statement that was very close to what the ERG leaders proposed. The bad news is one ERG leader received a call from the executive over her organization, apparently because he received a call from a C-Suite executive asking who this ERG leader was. At first, the executive offered support to help the ERG leader manage up. This offer of support was met with gratitude and thanks. But right before the call ended, the executive said, "You know you might be doing a great job with your ERG role, but if you are not doing your day job, you won't have a job."

After the initial shock wore off, she asked if there was something else the executive needed to discuss. She hadn't heard about any issues with her day job performance, including her last performance review. The executive said there was nothing else, and the call ended. Two years later, this ERG leader was suddenly laid off as part of a "reorganization," but she knew exactly when the target was put on her back. And she also knew that she would not have changed one thing she had done.

> *Before you pick your battles, make sure that you are willing to accept the consequences of your decision.*

> *Always do what's right and go out kickin' ass and taking names.*

Keeping People Engaged

Engagement is a lot easier as a leader if you make people feel heard and empowered. You probably accepted an ERG leadership role because someone made you feel wanted and empowered.

In addition to feeling heard and wanted, people need to know their input and time is important. This is where the rubber meets the road. If you make people feel heard (listening), wanted (we need you because…), they will feel valued and know their contributions matter.

How do you make people feel their input and time are valued? By recognizing them and saying thank you. I am not now (nor have I ever been) good at writing thank-you notes. My Mom tried hard to teach me the importance of writing thank-you notes, but I am just not good at it. However, I did learn the importance of saying thank you and put my own spin on it.

Saying thank you directly to someone is very impactful but saying thank you to that same person in front of others impacts at a whole new level. But you shouldn't do this just to do it. If you aren't authentic in your appreciation, then it can do more damage than if you hadn't said thank you at all.

Ways to thank people with impact can include:

- Sending them a thank you email and copying their manager.
- Having time during ERG meetings or having a specific meeting dedicated to recognition. As a leader, you can use this time to recognize people, but make sure to open it up so that others can give the gift of recognition.
- Utilize reward programs within your company to publicly say thank you and recognize ERG leaders and members.

Giving Away Confidence

Giving away confidence is something only a real leader can do. I am guessing your next question is, "How do you give away confidence?" There are easy ways to do this. If you do it with sincerity, the results will astound you.

As a leader, you know that being successful is not something you do alone. As the saying goes, teamwork makes the dream work. I try very hard to make sure when I am talking to someone, emailing, or texting, I always start with something positive and always end with something positive, like a thank you.

People that work with me will tell you that I LOVE the word awesome...so much so that I created a new word, or at least I think it's a new word...*awesomest*. And spell check just confirmed that this is a new word with a lovely red squiggly line underneath it. I use this word because I truly believe in people's awesomeness. And if people believe they are awesome to the point they know it's true, how confident do you think they will be? I don't mean just in the ERG work they do, but in work they do for the company and how they show up in life. And guess what? People who feel confident want to make other people feel awesome and so on and so on and so on.

The most important point to remember is to be authentic. You can't make people feel extraordinary and confident unless that is how you see them. If someone is working hard or hardly working, you must be honest with them about what you see and, at the same time, ask how you can help. People are more likely to be honest with someone if they feel valued and know they can be authentic and real. You can only create that kind of space if you are willing to listen and model authenticity.

> *Make it your mission to figure out how to make people awesome.*

The beauty of ERG leadership is that you have an opportunity to be yourself and impact the culture at your company. This creates a culture where everyone can bring their whole selves to work. Being an authentically passionate leader helps you to realize the potential, not only within yourself but within others. Working together, you can make an authentic impact on the lives of so many others. What more significant legacy is there?

Chapter 28 – Following My Own Advice

Dear ERG Leader:

Thank you! You have taken on a role that can have a long-term impact on your organization's culture and the lives of so many people. You might never know how much you positively impacted someone's life.

You are balancing your day job responsibilities with your ERG responsibilities, and you are doing a great job! There will be days where you don't feel balanced. That's ok. Achieving balance is not a destination; it is a way of being. I hope that my book will empower you to create more balance between your day job and your ERG job.

When you are feeling defeated, please pick up this book and re-read this chapter. I have been in your shoes and want you to know how vital your ERG work is.

You are amazing! You are putting your energy and focus on making your workplace, community, and world better. There is no higher calling as a human being.

Always remember, this work is important and impactful. Take care of yourself and go out and change the world.

With great respect,

Aimee Broadhurst

P.S. I would love to hear from you. Let me know how you are using my book or how things are going with your ERGs. Feel free to share your success stories or lessons learned from something that was not so successful. CoachAimee@InclusiveSpace.com

Acknowledgments

I will admit that I put off writing this part of my book because saying thank you doesn't seem like enough for the people in my life who have made this book possible. But here it goes.

First, I want to thank my husband and life partner, Trey. Without you, this book would not be possible. You have always believed in me, even when I didn't believe in myself. You have pushed me and called me out when needed, but most importantly, you have loved me unconditionally. And if all this were not enough, you edited my first complete draft of this book's manuscript, which made the final version a reality. I love you forever and ever, Amen!

My two daughters, Lauren and Kennedy. Thank you for supporting me, especially when it seemed like I might be losing my marbles. I love you both beyond measure, and you both inspire me to be a better Mom and human.

My sisters, Kristy and Kellie, thanks for believing in me when things got tough in May of 2018. Kristy, thanks for talking me through the times when I thought I couldn't finish this book and for encouraging me to start Inclusive Space. And to my Dad, thanks for believing in me and being excited as things continue to unfold.

My tribe from my time at Bank of America deserves a huge thank you: Jill, Rick, Shy, Crystal, Haley, Daniel, Patrick, and Jeff. I learned so much from each of you and value your friendships beyond measure. The amazing work we did together was the inspiration for this book and my next career.

Crystal Howard-Doliber is my sister from another mister. I cannot imagine having co-led LGBT Pride with anyone else, and this book would not have been written without you. We did incredible ERG work together, and I hope our good work will live on through this book.

Daniel Docherty, I cherish our friendship more than words can express. The Ally Program we built is our legacy. We will never know the number of people our program helped to feel safe to bring their whole selves to work. Your presence in my life is something for which I will always be grateful.

A huge thank you to my friend and champion of ERGs, Anna Ettin. I could not have finished this book without your support and your guidance. Thank you for reviewing, editing, and encouraging.

How I got lucky enough to have Alyssa Dver come into my life, I will never know. We connected through a mutual acquaintance, and during our first phone call, we both knew this would be a special relationship that would change both our lives. Thanks for bringing me into the ERG Leadership Alliance but more importantly, thank you for being my soul sister, my friend, and my encourager. You are a huge reason I finished this book and am now living out my life's purpose.

I am lucky to have two other people in my life, my friends and Inclusive Space™ partners in crime, Jeff White and Annaliese Parker. I cherish the friendship we have built and your encouragement, especially early on in this process, pushed me to keep going and make this book a reality. Annalise, I look forward to what we will do in the future with Allies for All.

I have worked with some amazing executive sponsors in my ERG life. There are two, in particular, I want to thank: Mark Stephanz and Gerry Stone. Mark and Gerry were the kind of executive sponsors every ERG leader hopes to have. They both had such a passion for the ERG and its mission and vision and were willing to help carry the load. Mark and Gerry, thank you for always having our backs as ERG leaders.

Mike Bloch and Kevin England, thank you for recognizing my passion and inviting me into ERG leadership.

A huge thank you to my book coach Cathy Fyock and all the authors I have met through her workshops and group calls. You have been my cheerleaders and encouragers. Amy Waninger, thank you for being an especially vocal cheerleader and for helping me get back to this book as the one I needed to write right now.

And finally, thank you to everyone doing Diversity & Inclusion and Employee Resource Group work. You are why I do the work I do, and I know that together we will continue to make the world a more Inclusive Space, one space at a time.

Made in the USA
Las Vegas, NV
18 March 2022